Collected Poems

Collected Poems

Robert Rendall

Edited by John Flett Brown
and Brian Murray

Steve Savage
LONDON AND EDINBURGH

Steve Savage Publishers Ltd
The Old Truman Brewery
91 Brick Lane
LONDON
E1 6QL

www.savagepublishers.com

Published in Great Britain by Steve Savage Publishers Ltd 2012
Copyright © the Estate of Robert Rendall 1946, 1951, 1957, 1966, 2012

ISBN: 978-1-904246-36-7

Typeset by Steve Savage Publishers
Printed and bound by SRP Ltd, Exeter

MIX
Paper from
responsible sources
FSC® C014540
FSC
www.fsc.org

Contents

Orkney Variants & Other Poems

Contents

Shore Poems

The Hidden Land

THE HIDDEN LAND

EASTERN WINDOW

Newly Collected Poems

Contents

Contents

Notes on the Poems

Introduction

ROBERT RENDALL, 24 January 1898 – 8 June 1967.

By all accounts – those of people who knew him or were familiar with his work in a variety of areas – Robert Rendall was a person of remarkable talent and versatility. A committed member of the Christian Brethren, poet, critic, essayist, antiquarian, artist, crofter and expert on the creatures of Orkney's shores, he was always busy at one or several of his interests, pursuing them actively or sharing ideas and discoveries through personal acquaintance and correspondence. Always, his religious faith, and activities to explain and promote it, were his first concern, but he gained recognition from specialists in all his fields for the work he did, while his publications made his ideas and findings accessible to wider audiences than the scholars and practitioners he studied and consulted.

The main details of Rendall's crowded life are widely known. For the purposes of this book, we have listed many of its occupations, but we must take one fact as pointing to his character and achievement: the man who gained honours, popularity and affection for the way he lived his life and what he produced in it, was thirteen years old when his formal education ended...

Brief Survey of Rendall's Poetry

Valuing friendship, respecting people of different – or no – persuasion, Rendall was influenced fundamentally by a higher motive:

> Noo ken I that there's Ane abune
> Can wheep away the monarch's croun,
>   An' wi' a gentler hand
>   Can Mercy's task command.

(1952)

Not all Rendall's religious poetry is as accessible or convincing as that, but, not surprisingly, his faith is a major source of his inspiration.

As John Allan outlined in a splendid essay, Rendall's view of "timelessness" was not easy to reconcile with accepted Brethren opinion. For example, the last stanza of "Cragsman's Widow" seemingly evokes the continuity of Nature as human beings come and go:

> Yet the sun shines doun on a' thing.
>   The links are bonnie and green,
> An' the sea keeps ebban an' flowan
>   As though it had never been.

(1951)

Although he had been trying his hand at poetry since his teens, Rendall was 48 when he published *Country Sonnets* in 1946, the first of his four volumes of verse. It was so well received that a reprint was called for after a fortnight. The blurb made his intentions clear: "*These poems seek to interpret against an Orcadian background the perennial urge in man's heart towards a life in the country, and reaffirm that without some share in work on the land, the pattern of country living is incomplete."* More loftily, *"they express the revolt of the human spirit against the repression of our modern mechanistic civilisation."*

The book's most successful poem was only ten lines long. It started:

Aald Jeems o' Quoys, wha erst wi' leid and line
Keen as a whitemaa, reaped the Rousay Soond,
And in his weathered yawl a twalmonth syne
Set lapster-creels the Westness craigs aroond...

(The Fisherman)

Hailed by George Mackay Brown as "a perfect poem", this stands out from the competent but occasionally uninspiring bulk of *Country Sonnets and Other Poems*. As Rendall was first to admit, the influence of his favourite Georgian poets can be too easy to identify. There was evidence of some successful assimilation, as in "In a Churchyard", with its suggestion of Housman's pastoral nostalgia and the attractively gritty awkwardness of Hardy. Other pieces showed Rendall's affection for sea and shore and the people living by their work on these elements, notably "Orkney Crofter" and "The Knowe".

These aspects were present abundantly in Rendall's next volume, *Orkney Variants and Other Poems* (1951), half the poems being in dialect, a medium on which he had strong opinions: *"The margin between superlative use of the vernacular and excessive sentimentality is so thin... that few seem able always to keep on the safe side of the line."*

To him, *"simplicity of diction, sincerity, colloquial truth and craftsmanship"* were essential. Rendall harnessed these qualities to his vision of Birsay to produce nearly a score of memorable works.

"Cragsman's Widow", "By wi' the Sea", "Salt i' the Bluid" and "The Planticru" are notable for their pictorial suggestions and the use of native words communicates tone and mood.

These poems appear effortless on the page, but the final versions were worked hard for, with many changes and revisions.

The section "Orkney Variants" comprises Rendall's demonstration that the motives of classical poetry can be identified in Birsay. Jeems and Willie of "Doun at the P'lace" were real, well-known folk in the village, while the croft interior in "The Happy Isle" and relation of the cosmic to the parochial in "Celestial Kinsmen" are statements of recognizable Birsay crofters having their lives and work recognised as part of the scheme of things:

Their lowan e'en are taakan tent
O' chiels like Mansie o' the Bu'
Whase days upon the land are spent
Ruggan wi' Taurus and the Pleugh.

There is a distinct improvement in the quality of the poems in English, "The Kelp-Worker" and "Erling's Rune" portraying very different experiences without sentimentality.

Similarly, "Old Jeems" in Rendall's third book, *Shore Poems* (1957) remains in the mind for its contrast between the settled, earthbound community of Birsay and the kingdom of the sea creatures.

A few concise character sketches in English and the Tennysonian "Last Voyage", a strong religious affirmation and Rendall's finest sonnet, "Renewal", are all we need note further, at this stage. Reversion to Standard English throughout was a disappointment to many, since, however vivid the descriptive or narrative detail, something of the character created by that "voice" was, inevitably, lost.

Shore Poems is evidence that Rendall was right in declaring: *"To confine oneself to English ... may ensure intelligibility to a wider public, but the innerly feeling of the old native life that still persists here and there, is not communicated..."*

Rendall's fourth volume of poems, *The Hidden Land*, was published in 1966. It was a triumph of spirit over illness to bring out the book a few months before his death. The voices of Wordsworth and Muir can be heard in pleasant-enough descriptive pieces, but the most interesting item is a series of short poems, "Eastern Window", significantly subtitled "Experiments in Haiku". Rendall was still attempting new challenges.

Perhaps enough of Robert Rendall's best verse has been quoted to illustrate his gifts. It seems a large claim to make, on the strength of a score of dialect poems, but those works can stand comparison with the lyrics of Hugh MacDiarmid – widely respected as the high-water mark of that genre in Scotland.

Rendall's other interests and the publications stemming from them will still appeal to the specialist, but the poems should gain him readers for the next forty years, with this collection offering many "new" pieces beside the contents of the first four books.

Inspiration, Feeling and Form

So various and abundant are Robert Rendall's works – in books, dispersed in newspapers and magazines or awaiting publication from manuscript and typescript – that it would require a book-length critical study to analyse and assess his literary productions with the thoroughness they deserve. Similarly, the range of his interests is so extensive as to call for a biography chronicling their origins, development and legacy.

These considerations are outwith the scope of the present volume, and can be given only summary treatment here. A proper investigation would not be just a matter of looking at Rendall's writing on a number of discrete subjects in turn, for frequently one area of subject-matter informs or feeds off another: thus, description of landscape can lead to comments on Society or religious affirmation; study of natural history may modulate into meditation on evolution, while reflection on the weaponry of modern times occasions trenchant condemnation of its scale and effects. References to visual art, a lifelong recreation of Rendall's, find their way into several poems, to provide convincing suggestions of scenic detail and mood at the same time as a resonance is created between those aspects of Rendall's experience and the inspiration of great painters[1]. And of course, the overtly religious works celebrating the motives and conduct of long-departed personalities are considering values and impulses animating Rendall himself.

It is impossible to explore these themes in detail here, but it does seem to us that we ought to provide a few passages of previously unavailable writing to illustrate how Rendall communicated his vision and beliefs as he explored the themes which most occupied him throughout a long working life. The subjects which bulked largest in his imagination and, certainly, in this book, were: his religion; a sense of the Orkney readership; native scenes, past and present, natural history and people; language – sonnets, dialect, "variants", the Lallans/"Plastics" controversy.

"God's steadfast purpose see"

While Rendall devoted much of his time over many years to the pursuit and study of literature, with consistent concern for the widest possible circulation and appraisal

---

1. Examples abound: Neil Dickson's essay (2012) draws attention to "a number of ways in which Rendall sought for the interpenetration of his various interests".

of his own poems, together with an understandable aspiration for recognition by critics of standing outwith Orkney, he never lost sight of where his priority lay:

> There are pleasures which in themselves are good and beautiful, such as books, art, poetry, nature study, or conversation. These ought to be regarded as tokens of God's kindness, and we, recognizing their transitory nature, are not to hold them as aims of existence. Otherwise they will usurp the position that God alone is intended to fill.[2]

We imagine that most authors who produce a substantial body of work can be seen to have fallen short of their own – and others' – expectations and standards, from time to time. Rendall was not an exception. Two most helpful essays bring out aspects of how his Brethren unpbringing and subsequent adherence to that faith could seem at variance with poetry in which he dwelled on the observable continuity of patterns – belief and behaviour – after significant events. Then there was what was condemned as faulty technique, "*characteristic of the worst Brethren hymnodical tradition*"[3] in which he had grown up. "*His dislike of literary modernism meant that for his religious poetry he turned to an outmoded poetics.*"[4]

Theology apart, it is not difficult to find examples of tortuous syntax eking out rhythm or rhyme; over-fondness for exclamatory phrases; employment of familiar imagery long past its original fresh appropriateness and so on, in Rendall's religious poems, particularly some of the earliest ones, but there are many whose technical assurance, lucidity and pervasive engagement

---

2. D 27/1/4 Robert Rendall, "An Account of the Birth of this Diary" (begun on 20 February 1918).

3. John Allan, "Robert Rendall", *Aware*, 70/5, May 1991, p21.

4. Neil T. R. Dickson, "Littoral Truth: The Mind of Robert Rendall (1898–1967), to be published later in 2012 as an expanded version of a paper presented at the Orkney Science Festival, 6 September, 1998.

with the subject make us question his own assertions that he had been unable to compose poetry which was a successful embodiment of his beliefs, to match the accomplishment of his best "secular" creations:

> My only answer is, 'When standing on that rock I worship Heaven's God at Nature's shrine'. (1916–17)

> 'Bring them to Me!' The voice of One whose hand
>   Dropped down the manna with the morning dew,
> In ancient days was sounding through the land. (1927)

> Dull clerks, know this, men are not made of stone,
> Nor, spite of labour, live by bread alone. (1949)

Here, the immediacy of personal experience or observation, an expression of belief and a forthright statement are evoked, and these extracts have many successful counterparts in the poet's treatment of spiritual beliefs and actions.

"Writing for our own folk"

> ...in Orkney we still have a community which is conscious of itself as a single whole – a sort of big family, of which we are all proud to be members ...Writers who address an unknown public cannot have the same satisfaction that we have here in Orkney of writing for our own folk whom we meet with day by day...[5]

In his own day, Robert Rendall was a well-known figure in Kirkwall, at his "retreat" in the parish of Birsay, and latterly Stromness, respected for his antiquarian finds and the commentaries he wrote on them, for the poems and essays he contributed to the local newspapers and, above all, for his descriptions of scenes and people, that Orcadians regarded as authentic transcripts of life in their area. (That a fair number of them were in Orkney dialect, depicting actual people whom readers could

5. Robert Rendall, in conversation with Ernest Marwick, 1962.

recognize and relate to, was much to the community's satisfaction, while the appearance of his "Orkney Variants" in newspapers before the book of that title was issued, deepened their appreciative response.)

The poet was always on the lookout for evidence of working practices and attitudes, both present and past, which accounts for the number of poems written ("mentally", he would say) on the bus, or reflecting on bygone conditions as recorded in books:

> They talked of this and that, were ready to discuss
> The smacks discharging at the harbour head,
>   Weather and price of crops, and foreign wars,
>   Or how the wedding went, and who was dead… (1959)

This re-creation of business and conversation among "our own folk" is set in the Kirkwall of 1759, but it is as vividly suggestive as another one in which Rendall savoured his view of country folk's activity as the car in which he was a passenger sped between the fields:

> Country women, old men with bowed backs,
> Lifting their tatties, and into sacks
> Filling heaped pailfuls… (1951)

Hard work and social contacts in each case, and Time's progress doing nothing to obscure motives, all make Rendall's conclusion an irresistible one:

> These nameless ghosts, our fabled ancestors,
> Were they at all so different from us?

"The secret locus of the happy life"

If such continuity of behaviour among his acquaintances in town and parish was very much to a mature Rendall's taste, their physical surroundings were of equally lasting stability and delight to him from his pre-teen years, when he was

21

drawn towards awareness of the natural environment. In time, increased understanding of this generated appreciation which developed into an abiding passion:

> Blind when a boy, yet seeing cliff and wave
> I knew not that my spirit was being bound
> By invisible threads, of sight and sound and air
> To chain my spirit to this alien land...[6]

One place had a special fascination for him:

> Localities associated with childhood retain strange fascination over the mind in after years, haunting us...with a mysterious penumbra of memory and feeling. They invoke a sense of timeless tranquillity, as if at long last we had found for ourselves the secret locus of the happy life. An atmosphere surrounds them, indefinable but strongly realised, of ineffable peace. With every return to the old haunts returns also the old irrational joy and speechless contentment. Such a place, to me, is Birsay.[7]

At times, the "old haunts" did not appear such an idyllic setting, for the onset of coarse weather could send huge waves rampaging towards the shore under a darkened sky, while Rendall's spare-time home felt shaken to the foundations when a gale got up. That did not matter to the poet, who made the testing experience into language of appropriate vigour, visual appeal and symbolic portent – when he was not capturing it in paintings[8]:

> With gaping jaws this sharp-toothed Orkney strand
> Snatches in greedy haste the ocean's hand.   (1957)

While the rocks and inlets which appear so frequently in Rendall's work already had historical associations, perhaps his most memorable characters are so, because they immortalised

6. D27/2/10 (2): typescript by Robert Rendall.

7. D 27/2/6: typescript by Robert Rendall.

8. For example, "A wild day on the Birsay Coast", in the Orkney Library Archive.

for the community people who lived and worked in it, popular for their combination of hard work and social qualities, examples to counter George Mackay Brown's statement:

> But the people who bear the weight of history always are those whose names survive only on churchyard stones, the peasant and the fisherman.[9]

If the brief characterisations of certain people in *Shore Poems* (pp127–8 in this volume) and the reference to "the honoured guest" in "Burgess Ticket" (p129 in this volume) enshrined the interests and natures of folk so well-known to Kirkwall residents, that they did not require to be named, Rendall ensured that the Jeems and Willie/Billy of his Birsay poems were given a place in their parish history which is likely to outlive "the lettered kirkyard stone". In their own day, everyone could supply surnames for the pair, while in ours Rendall's *Orkney Shore* (1960) and periodical contributions have been supplemented by a splendid book, illuminating the work and leisure in Willie Harvey's life[10].

Sonnets

Willie, Jeems, the peat worker, the cragsman's widow, the old straitsman and others are presented crisply in Rendall's poems, exemplifying a form which he admired and emulated:

> Those cameo-like poems in the Greek Anthology that present a world in miniature – a world peopled with shepherds and fishermen and lovers, standing sharp against a pastoral background ... A single moment is caught, symbolising some fundamental aspect of man's life. The effect is, literally, graphic...[11]

9. "The Literature of the Northern Islands", BBC, Autumn 1973.

10. *Willie's World – 1959*, transcription of his diary, with commentary by Gregor Lamb and contributions by a number of relatives, friends and dedicated supporters of the project.

11. Rendall's Introduction to *A Book of Scottish Sonnets*, unpublished, D 27/2/2, p26.

It is evident from his four books that Rendall had profited from study of the "tightness" he saw as a feature of poems by writers in that Anthology; Hardy and Housman, too, he followed at times, with admirable compression of content, stripping events to the barest essentials without losing continuity and power of statement as his portraits developed until "The Fisherman", "Orkney Crofter", "The Twa", "Erling's Rune" and several of his short memorials of contemporary figures achieved a sculptured, monumental effect.

In our "Newly Collected" section the influence of earlier, classical writers can be identified in the spirit, language and structure of "The Sceptic", "The Morning's Wark" and "Willie's Boat", but overall where his work responds to a place's features, atmosphere and people it is the sonnet that dominates. It is no wonder that Rendall, finding the form's discipline to his liking, employed it repeatedly in those works that have survived from his early – *i.e.* pre-*Country Sonnets* – period, a time when he was studying poetic genres and established masterpieces as preparation for his own literary development:

> Excellence in the sonnet, it would seem, has almost invariably been attained through discipline in classical studies and expert craftsmanship in metrical forms.[12]

And given that Rendall found the *Greek Anthology*[13] poems congenial to his taste and standards, his taking to the sonnet for so many poems of place was a logical –

12. Introduction to *A Book of Scottish Sonnets*, D 27/2/2, page 9.

13. *The Greek Anthology* consists of between 6,000 and 7,000 poems, 4,000 from two collections made in Constantinople in the 10th and the 14th centuries, the remainder found by later scholars of literature and monuments' inscriptions. The earliest one dated from 700BC, the collection continuing to 1000AD.

perhaps inevitable – step:

> They [the Greek Anthology works] have always been happily followed in the sonnet.[14]

He set out to provide in his own sonnets and the later *Variants*

> ...that central imagination of the subject-matter which is so essential to a true poem...[15]

His pursuit of that ideal is consistent and frequently effective in poems evocative of time and place, owing much to his presentation of known characters. In Rendall's execution of his plan, scenic details are well integrated with accounts of the feelings of people living and working close to Nature, with its changing moods, people conducting themselves in "the secret locus of the happy life". The "single moment" from one age or generation to another impresses upon us the poet's fascination with the seemingly perpetual presence of elements appealing to a spirit prizing beauty of environment and, as he sees it, continuity of its natural features. These create an ambience whose charm, challenges and permanence are unaffected by the generations passing through, each to be succeeded by others animated by the motives and impulses of many nameless predecessors:

> Man comes and tills the field and lies beneath...(Tennyson)

Mansie o' the Bu', young Magnus wi' the muckle teeth, the sceptic and others portrayed by Rendall appear true to their nature in particular circumstances, but they are to be seen, also, *sub specie æternitatis*, for it is Rendall's

---

14. *Ibid.*, p25.

15. Letter from Rendall to James Fergusson, 30 April 1947, D 27/7/1

achievement to have demonstrated that

> ...the seas that beat so mournfully among the Aegean isles
> are those that thunder on our Atlantic seaboard...[16]

It is difficult to disagree with Rendall's conclusion, while recognizing the discomfort with which some of his commentators viewed it:

> Birsay has something of pagan timelessness in its atmosphere, and the sensitive mind may still in this secluded and unspoiled natural paradise
>
> > 'Have sight of Proteus rising from the sea
> > And hear old Triton blow his wreathed horn'.[17]

Dialect, variant and "the strife of tongues"

> The dialect used in these poems is a thin survival from the speech of the ancient Norse earldom, diluted by Scots' idioms and vocabulary, and now heard only in a context of common English.[18]

Rendall's note does not stir the blood. Nor does it instil a desire to engage with the poems as described, for the bald statements require "unpacking" by readers who may not have experience of the linguistic considerations that they raise. Tucked away at the back of the book, they can be overlooked, the reader left to go through the poems, with individual responses uncluttered by the technicalities of the "explanation".

Fortunately, the texts are as accessible in terms of understanding as Rendall's well-intentioned summary is unhelpful – as we see it. The dialect works present a number of characters whose language, philosophy and organisation bear comparison with the acclaimed "The

16. *A Book of Scottish Sonnets*, p27.

17. "Birsay", D 27/2/6.

18. Notes, *Orkney Variants and Other Poems* (1951), p63 (and this volume, p330).

Fisherman". Rendall felt he required to gloss only half a dozen of the poems about how Time tests a person's ability to understand and cope with the demands of bereavement, old age and solitary life. Of these, perhaps only a few local words might puzzle non-Orcadians then or today, for, as Hugh Marwick acknowledged in many of his definitions in *The Orkney Norn*,[19] words and expressions he traced back to the old language can be in everyday use, south and further afield, while Rendall's choice of vocabulary within well-evoked contexts helps to reduce the difficulty non-Scots might encounter from time to time.

Such an occasion might be when reading "Mansie's Threshing", a long ballad whose farming environment and activity necessitate the use of words associated with these specialist aspects, but even here credible characterisation, pace of narrative and sustained supernatural interest make for readers' comprehension of "twart-backs,…minted,… soople" and a few other markers of scene and function. Nevertheless we have offered a number of glosses for reasons given in the first note, page 325.

"Shore Tullye" is worthy of mention as an example of Rendall's love of experiment. Simon W. Hall's elegant analysis of its aims and metrics is persuasive[20] – which would have pleased the poet, who described it as "a *tour de force*",[21] the praise he had given the earlier "Scarabrae Re-Visited".[22] That witty, but not trivialising "tour" of

---

19. (1929)

20. *The History of Orkney Literature*, John Donald, for Birlinn Ltd., 2010, pp121–22.

21. Draft typescript of a letter from Rendall to Tom Scott, D 27/5/8/2, in reply to Scott's letter of 23 January 1965: "I was particularly pleased at your inclusion of Shore Tullye which because of its intricate metrical structure was something of a *tour de force*" (referring to *The Oxford Book of Scottish Verse*, edited by Scott).

22. *Country Sonnets & Other Poems*, 1946, pp45–48 (and this volume pp74–76).

Orkney's most famous and visited archaeological feature, is very different from "An experiment in Scaldic metre" in tone and prosody, but both poems are faithful to the writer's chosen modes. Not content with what was evidence of Rendall's ear and imagination enabling him to "reconstruct" historical episodes, he was anything but finished with the study and employment of different metres and forms. Having devoted much time to cultivating "the Sonnet's scanty plot", Rendall had a number of samples and trials to occupy him, but first was the form of composition in which he had made an arresting start...

Pressed by James Fergusson to produce more poems in the dialect which had brought "The Fisherman" local acclaim, Rendall looked out pieces he had not included in *Country Sonnets*, in addition to taking up the request to go on with more:

> It may interest you to know which poems in my book have caught the public imagination *here* ... there have been two which seem to have captured everyone – Birsay, and The Fisherman...[23]

Rendall was considering the potentiality of dialect:

> Translations, I am beginning to find out, lend themselves well to such treatment.[24]

Mulling over Edwin Muir's statement on there being a "linguistic division" between Scots' thoughts and feelings, he felt that translation did not present that problem, for, while a translator had to change atmosphere "*and make something new, however literal his translation*", a great deal of the "*imagination and mental thought*" was given him or her by the original writer.

23. D 27/7/1 Letter from Rendall to Fergusson, 25 April 1947.

24. Ibid., Letter to Fergusson, 30 April 1947.

There is a familiar ring to Rendall's note at the end of his *Orkney Variants* volume:

> These Variants are not strict verbal translations, but transpose into an Orkney setting poems whose foreign originals depict some universal aspect of life.[25]

It is helpful to have Rendall's development of the point in a Scottish context:

> Translation may not always have been verbally strict according to modern standards, but the timeless and universal note in the original has not infrequently been given a typically Scottish setting. The wine-jar of the Mediterranean has become the milk-jar of the Scottish pastoral.[26] Little is lost and much is gained in such transliteration of local "properties" which involve no sacrifice of the central poetic idea. Poems in this manner might well bear some such formal name as "variant", which would seem more strictly to define what is meant here than does "variation".[27]

This passage can be put beside Rendall's "Variants" as a yardstick of how he achieved his aims. The copy of poems sent with this letter to James Fergusson, we would identify as D 27/2/10, "Scots Variations on the Greek Anthology": while early versions of "Envy", "Plain Fare: Guid Lear" and (*pace* Rendall's forgetting he had altered it) "The Fisherman" we assign to the late 1920s, their being typed on the same kind of card as others influenced by the Greek Anthology, notably "The Sailor's Knowe", which was dated

25. Cf Introduction to *A Book of Scottish Sonnets*, p26, discussed from p24 above.

26. Cf "The Twa", *Orkney Variants*, p92 below.

27. D 27/2/7 "Dialect – The Literary Use of Dialect" – working typescript of an essay by Rendall; James Fergusson praised "your variants from the Greek Anthology", following his receipt of poems sent him by Rendall on 18 August 1947 (and again on 24 March 1948, "your Orkney Variants…" and "Cragsman's Widow". We agree with Neil Dickson (op. cit. p119) that the essay was in progress during 1947.

"17 2 27", with an attractive sketch, almost twenty years before it appeared as "The Knowe" in *Country Sonnets*. Interestingly, those versions were untitled. A later version of the poem that became known as "The Fisherman" was called "The Sailor's Grave", the title written over the typescript headed "Variation from the Greek Anthology", followed by "Adapted from Lang's translation of", which points to Rendall's method. Similarly notable are the three attempts he made before being satisfied with "Celestial Kinsmen", his revisions of "The Twa" and other poems, the last-mentioned differing from its original stimulus according to the poet's "Variant" theory.

That designation applies to theme, as well as language and ethos: Rendall's putting the accent and milieu of contemporary Orkney in place of those embodying features of different societies brought him to adaptations of texts in several languages either via translations by others, or his own, without loss of the virtues the older works possess.

We are convinced that Rendall's best-known poems are some – if not all – of the fifteen short pieces printed in *Orkney Variants & Other Poems* under the headings "Poems in Dialect" and "Orkney Variants" (six and nine, respectively). Yet, these comprise only 146 lines, averaging just under ten lines each. When we consider that the poem which enthused his public more than most others had been written some twenty years before it was published in book form[28] and that a few others set aside

---

28. In a letter to James Fergusson, dated 23 April 1947, the poet included "The Fisherman" in the list of "early" lyrics, written between 1926 and 1930, informing Fergusson that it had not been altered for *Country Sonnets* – eliciting the comment in Fergusson's reply of 28 April, "There is to me something very suggestive in the fact that of the 1926–1930 poems in your book the only one you have not revised, and therefore presumably felt to be as good as you could make it, is 'The Fisherman', the only poem in the book in dialect."

when *Country Sonnets* was issued were not released for nearly three decades, it seems a wonder that the little collection appearing in *Orkney Variants* succeeded in finding its way between hard covers. It is surprising that Rendall did not apply himself much more to a mode in which good judges held him to excel, which would have delighted those admiring the dialect/variant works.

The "Plastics" Controversy

> Take ... the school of young and youngish poets now writing the kind of artificial Scots which I presumed to label 'plastic' – it will be a long time before they forgive me![29]

James Fergusson's extolling Rendall's poems, putting the review of books by a number of poets in his way – several being by "Plastics" – was bound to promote adverse criticism of the Orkney-based writer (from poets denigrated by Fergusson, who saw writing in Scots as a political gesture or statement, raising fears of Scottish nationalism). In fact, the "Synthetic Scots" was meant to be a build-up of all the linguistic resources available within the country, a synthesis from which the new poets could select what suited them, rather than an artificial, "made-up" language.

Fergusson was accused of gross exaggeration when he compared Rendall to Wordsworth. Maurice Lindsay excoriated the author of *Orkney Variants & Other Poems* in his review, seeing

> ... no vestige of originality, and therefore no genuine merit in any of Mr Rendall's English pieces. They lie dead on the

29. James (later Sir James) Fergusson. He was editor of *The Glasgow Herald*'s Week-End Page, before going on to be Keeper of the Records of Scotland, and did much to promote Rendall's work and reputation from the beginning of a correspondence between them, initiated by the good offices of Stanley Cursiter, at Rendall's request. Unfailingly helpful, Fergusson praised the poet on radio and in the newspaper, offering comments and advice, while making no secret of his dismissing those he had designated "Plastics".

paper, crouched in the heroic attitudes that older poets adopted with success when alive.[30]

To his credit, however, Lindsay, whose opinions carried weight in literary circles, found it

> ...a different story when we come to consider Mr Rendall's pieces in the Orkney tongue. Here are many delightful things – the 'Variants' themselves...and a number of local sketches of personalities and places. For these, then, this book should be bought by all lovers of Orkney.

Rendall himself discussed the "Plastics", reviewed them and wrote a number of poems poking fun at them – not printed until now – but he had good relations with Douglas Young, the most prominent writer among those espousing the cause of Synthetic Scots: referred to in complimentary terms by Young in his anthology, *Scottish Poetry 1851–1951*[31], Rendall had two poems printed in it.

The extensive bibliography of the Plastics debate reveals that Rendall was regarded as an Establishment figure, with a platform from which he could attack the poets writing in Scots. His reviews were models of the genre – scholarly, well-informed, beautifully written and impressively analytical. Yet the praise from Fergusson did him few real favours. Although his own poems coming out in the *Herald*'s Week-End Page offered readers an opportunity to enjoy his best work to date, Rendall risked being stereotyped as a "regional" poet, remote in place and spirit from the metropolitan "Plasticists".[32]

30. "Orkney and Ireland", *The Scots Review*, July 1951.

31. Douglas Young, 1952, Thomas Nelson

32. The bibliography of "Plastic Scots" is extensive. Most convenient and a fine treatment of what was a contentious issue in its day, is Trevor Royle's *A Time for Tyrants* (2011).

Why a Collected Poems?

> "Probably his work would have gained in repute had those poems been carefully sifted and the best published as 'Selected Poems'. Collection is rarely justified except when inferior poems are accepted as side-notes to more solid achievement, as with long-established national poets..."[33]

Robert Rendall's comments on another writer's *Collected Poetical Works* sound uncompromising. While there may be a nod towards the printing of certain poems by major writers as signposts on the way to creditable, accomplished productions, his statement seems to dismiss the value of presenting the bulk of others' publications, including juvenilia, *jeux d'esprit*, false starts and changes of tack in theme or structure on the journey towards a developed world-view and a method of communicating it. "Long-established national poets", however, are few.

Many who knew Rendall or have read his voluminous correspondence[34] will know that his attitude was anything but discouragingly elitist. Rendall's nature was to recognise and make the best of what others produced in any sphere while applying rigorous standards to his own work.

He did contemplate a *Selected Poems* of his own, listing most of the titles from his four slim volumes, grouped thematically. Rendall spent much time on the choice and arrangement, but the project remained unpublished[35]. While a chronological plan was ruled out, the proportion of poems selected and the headings under which he placed them illustrated his concern to have a substantial part of his *œuvre* in the public domain.

Whatever his doubts about the wisdom of publishing a writer's Collected Poems, he also saw the benefits of a

33. Robert Rendall, 30 December 1948 "Some new poetry"
34. The Orkney Library, Kirkwall: Archives D27
35. The Orkney Library, Kirkwall: Archives D27

33

year-by-year presentation. More in keeping with his known character and literary habits was his musing: "*There is something peculiarly satisfying in being able to chart a poet's progress from early work to mature poetic utterance...*"[36] That is a view which we have shared in preparing this compilation, and we have tried hard to put dates to his poems.

Further testimony to his enduring concern for the publication and presentation of his poetry was Rendall's issue of four volumes, his repeated assaults on seemingly intractable subjects and, in his last year, strong desire to see within covers a number of poems which are important examples of subject and treatment: "*I often wonder what I should do about my dozen or so later poems, unpublished in book form. They form a unity of feeling. 'The Hidden World' hits them off. At present they are lost except in the files of* The Glasgow Herald."[37]

And it would appear that Rendall had no fixed objection to a *Collected Poems* in principle, judging from his several penetrating reviews of poetry from different periods in *The Glasgow Herald* in the late 1940s.

It would of course have been possible for the present editors to have selected what they judged to be the best of Rendall's poems, published and unpublished, and to have put together a volume of Selected Poems, perhaps taking into account his own preparations for such a volume. Some of the poems in the present volume are unfinished, and some are not his best work. But tastes differ, and in the end we decided that the best approach was to lay Robert Rendall's work before the public and let them judge which of his poems are to be more highly regarded.

36. *The Glasgow Herald*, review of *Collected Poems* by Lilian Bowes Lyon.

37. Letter to E. W. Marwick, Kirkwall Archive 1966. "The Hidden World" appeared as a pamphlet of poems in time to serve as Rendall's last literature present for friends at Christmas, 1966, despite the poet's poor health, as *The Hidden Land.*

It is important that readers have opportunity to experience the work on which Rendall's current reputation rests, before including 177 hitherto inaccessible pieces in their considerations. While Rendall's first book, *Country Sonnets* (1946) was an immediate success, quickly reprinted twice, with the others received so well as to sell out in his lifetime, for many years his titles have been expensive items, appearing at sales infrequently and lost to the general public when purchased.

Apart from the Orkney Library, only a few institutions hold copies of one or other Rendall collection; occasionally a poem is quoted in a newspaper or anthology, or the writer is treated in a general survey; Orkney schools and the county's College, part of the University of the Highlands and Islands, are eager to afford him a place in their courses and activities, while different festivals and interest groups publicise and present readings. But lack of substantial reprints for people not involved as students or spectators and the difficulty of obtaining selections over several decades have led to Rendall's material and technique being distanced from a potential readership dependent on previous generations' assertions about their quality – prepared to accept them, but deprived of the facility to consult the originals.[38]

Fellow-poet George Mackay Brown had long considered Rendall's dialect poems remarkable: a typical statement in his later assessments of Rendall assured readers that one poem from *Country Sonnets* (1946), three from *Orkney Variants* (1951) "...and some dozen others"

38. A most welcome collection of a reasonable quantity and range of Rendall's poems was Neil Dickson's *An Island Shore – Selected Writings of Robert Rendall* (The Orkney Press, 1990) which contained 43 poems, comprising 540 lines.

were "…among the best poems that have been written in Scotland this [twentieth] century".[39]

Those who hoped for more dialect poems were disappointed when none were included in *Shore Poems* (1957) and *The Hidden Land* (1966). Alongside the highly-regarded dialect poems, his poetry in English tended to be regarded as somewhat old-fashioned, and Rendall was marginalised as a gifted curiosity outside mainstream writing. For anyone intending to read Rendall's poetry – whether admirers of his Orcadian content, or interested in his traditional English manner, or wishing to make their own judgements – his books were hard to find.

As time went on, critics who had deprecated aspects of Rendall's non-dialect poems softened their attitudes. George Mackay Brown, whose consistency of support for the Orcadian lyrics had been unswerving for more than forty years – the period for which he had reservations about most of the English poems' content and technique – expressed his community's need for reprints in an eloquent essay that made a point of praising some of the poems written in English: not only were people of mature years being denied an essential element of their Orkney culture; their children and generations after them looked like having little opportunity to find and develop interest in the body of Rendall's work:

> "It is extraordinary that a poet of such high endeavour and achievement has never been reprinted. It can't be allowed to continue, surely. We can't deprive young Orcadians of such life-enhancing rare delights."[40]

39. George Mackay Brown, "Reading Robert Rendall's Verse", *The Orcadian*, 24 September 1953, p2.

40. "Under Brinkie's Brae", *The Orcadian*, 14 September 1989, p4 (reprinted in *Rockpools and Daffodils*, Gordon Wright, Edinburgh, 1992).

Another factor inhibiting recognition of Rendall's status was his changing a number of apparently "achieved" texts. At first sight inexplicable, this distorted the structure or altered the language so significantly as to obscure or lose the conception embodied in technically competent poems. Several examples are extant, demonstrating how the poet's verbal modifications – words deleted, added to texts – far from improving them, could dilute colour, intensity and impact. Left in their original contexts, several would have been among the most attractive features of their volumes. As it is, to put what we see as better passages within readers' grasp, we have included them in the Notes, hoping that they will provide interesting supplements to poems in the main text.

In an earlier publication we rehearsed the familiar case for Rendall being "minor" in aspiration, scope and achievement, as evidenced by the 120 poems in his four volumes. The sheer number of "new" poems that we are able to include in this volume must call into question the accepted wisdom that has characterised Rendall's *œuvre* as essentially limited. Some of the poems printed here for the first time seem to have an interest, assurance and technical accomplishment as great as if not greater than some of those Rendall selected for publication.

No doubt pressure on space dictated some invidious choices by him, but his preparation of so many poems in manuscript or type and repeated reworkings are evidence of his reluctance to rest on the achievement represented by the four books. Now, in the light of the dates, content and artistic quality of so many additions to his canon, we can present a volume spanning Rendall's fifty years of recorded composition. It is our hope, too, that more poems have still to emerge from private collections or forgotten periodicals, until, instead of "Dialect poems still strong after 40 years",[41] four decades on, it will be agreed that this much bulkier, varied corpus of Robert Rendall's work will have found a secure place in the literature of Orkney, while appealing to the wide readership outside these islands:

> "Robert Rendall through his poetry still has friends to make, in the near and in the distant future..."[42]

"Where go the poet's lines? Speak from your folded papers!"[43]

While Rendall's four books were taken to contain all the work he considered worthy of publication in book form, the substantial number of poems we have collected for the final section demonstrate that he was constantly on the alert for subjects, images, characters to turn into poetic form when time for writing was afforded him.

Novelty of form was as important to him as the appearance of promising subjects he had not treated or developed before. While adding to his stock of sonnets Rendall continued to work on poems written over the years, but requiring modification as he saw it: ballads; "laureate" poems in which he saw himself as speaking for Orkney; an attempt at the Matter of Orkney in an ambitiously planned "Sea Symphony"; lyrics; pastiches of other authors; parody; limericks and whimsical pieces – some with a glimmering of deeper significance – and, in his last years, haiku occupied his attention and pen. Folded in yellowing heaps, blurred cuttings from newspapers, much-worked-upon typescripts and handwritten sheets,

---

41. "Dialect poems still strong after 40 years", *The Orcadian*, 16 June 2007, p23.
42. George Mackay Brown, *op. cit.*
43. Oliver Wendell Holmes, "The Poet's Lot".

or exquisite fair copies in notebook or diary – the uncollected works we present here seem to us "still fresh and old as time", new to our generation, but embodying the thoughts of Robert Rendall and the variety of forms he adopted to communicate them. We hope that readers will find the "new" poems a welcome surprise, while rejoicing in this first opportunity to read all Rendall's hitherto scarce books of poetry in one volume.

John Flett Brown
Brian Murray
Stromness, August 2012

NOTE ON THE TEXT

After Rendall's four books of poems, the *Newly Collected* texts are printed in a loosely thematic arrangement.

While we have adopted what we consider to be the poet's favoured version – generally, the latest – from evidence of date, stage of development, etc., we are reluctant to omit a number of alternatives and fragments, such as Rendall described: *pieces that have value as memoralia rather than uniform intrinsic value as poems*...Accordingly, we have placed them in the *Fragments* and *Textual Variants* sections. We have supplied titles for some poems, putting them within square brackets.

"Work in Progress"

ON AN ENGRAVING.

Of old engravings framed upon the wall
I chiefly love this bishop grave and wise;
A preacher he who kept the creed of Paul,
Nor winked at truth to favour royal eyes.
Much have I scanned of late the tufted beard,
The tight round cowl, the mien of serious grace;
Each time I look the more I hold revered
This holy man with virtue's modest face.
In calf-bound volume have I read his deep
And weighty discourse, preached with godly fear,
And well have marked how he in mind did keep
The under-shepherd's motto graven here:
"Sermons take not from men's applause renown;
The people's practice is the preacher's crown."

These facsimiles illustrate Rendall's readiness to review and change significantly a number of poems:

"To an Engraving of Bishop Reynolds" (pp 216 and 324); "Envy" (p91); "Plain Fare: Guid Lear" (p91); "Mac Pherson o' the Glen" (p165); "The Fisherman" (pp29–30, 68) and "The Knowe" (pp29–30, 72).

Acknowledgements

We are very grateful for the encouragement and help we have received from a number of individuals and institutions.

Mr Robert P. Rendall, nephew of the poet and his literary executor, has granted permission to quote from his uncle's work. In addition, we were pleased to be given copies of poems which have filled gaps and supplied dates. Many thanks for his kindness.

Mr Neil Dickson was most generous in letting us have the text of essays by him, including a long one due to be published soon. Unfailingly helpful comments, suggestions and copies of poems from Mr Bertie Harvey have put us in his debt, while the speed and value of responses to requests for information from Miss Tessa Spencer, Assistant Registrar, The National Archives of Scotland and Mr Graham Johnson, Christian Brethren Archivist, The John Rylands University Library, The University of Manchester, were startling.

We must pay tribute to the patience, knowledge and professional services of the Orkney Library staff during the years this book has been in preparation: Mr Gary Amos, Mrs Karen Walker and Mrs Maureen Drever. In the Orkney Archive, Misses Alison Fraser and Lucy Gibbon, Mrs Annie Manson, Mrs Sarah Jane Gibbon, Miss Sarah MacLean and Messrs David Mackie and Colin Rendall have ensured we enjoyed access to the resources we required to consult. We acknowledge with thanks their grasp of detail, width of reference and cheerful efficiency, as well as permission to quote from the Library and Archive's holdings. Mrs Rebecca Ford, Mrs Carol Flett and Mrs Christine Harcus made the Public Library, Stromness, a comfortable environment for study, writing and seeking information.

Mrs Mary Steer has been consistently kind and helpful, lending books and providing hospitality; Mrs Elizabeth Johnson lightened the task of tracking Rendall's publications by the loan of a significant number of items.

For the loan of a painting by Robert Rendall, and permission to reproduce it, we are indebted to Mrs Ruth Bain. Miss Lesley McLetchie's friendly copying of materials from the poet's work-sheets and fair copies was a most stimulating and heartening aid to our work, as was Dr Rowena Murray, Dr Morag Thow and Mr Howie Firth's reading a draft of the work. At no notice, Messrs Magnus Dennison, Peter K. I. Leith, Joe Laughton and Jocky Wood answered several questions, with obvious benefit to our understanding and approach.

Libraries outwith Orkney have been of great assistance: those of Edinburgh, Glasgow and Strathclyde Universities; the British Library; the Public Library (Carnegie) Ayr; Edinburgh Central Library; the Mitchell Library Glasgow and the National Library of Scotland.

Mrs Maureen Gray has produced masses of typed text with great speed and accuracy, while making time to offer helpful comments and advice. We thank her and anyone who has helped, but is not acknowledged here. All omissions of this kind will be rectified in any reprint.

We must include in the list of those who helped, our wives, Cynthia and Liza, without whose unfailing patience and support our work would not have proceeded as we wished.

Finally, Steve Savage, our publisher, has exhibited what we think are the ideal qualities required by authors eager to have their book presented to the public: knowledge of the subject matter, appreciation of design and concern over detail.

Select Bibliography

(a) Works by Robert Rendall:

Country Sonnets & Other Poems, Kirkwall (1946).

A Book of Scottish Sonnets, unpublished (1946–49).

Extracts from a Travel Diary, 1950, Kirkwall (1950).

Orkney Variants & Other Poems, Kirkwall, (1951).

History, Prophecy and God, London, The Paternoster Press (1954).

The Greatness and Glory of Christ, London, Pickering and Inglis (1956).

Mollusca Orcadensia, reprint, Proceedings of the Royal Society of Edinburgh (1956).

Shore Poems and other Verse, Kirkwall (1957).

Extracts from a Travel Diary, 1957–58, Kirkwall (1959).

Orkney Shore, Kirkwall (1960).

The Hidden Land, Kirkwall (1966).

(b) About Rendall:

Allan, John, 'Robert Rendall', *Aware* 70/5 (May 1991).

Brown, George Mackay, 'Orcadian Classical Poetry / Mr Robert Rendall's "Country Sonnets"', *The Orkney Herald*, 17 December 1946.

— 'Robert Rendall, A Modern Orkney Poet', *The New Shetlander*, 11, August–September 1948.

— 'War of Words', *The Orkney Herald*, 2 May 1950.

— 'A New Book of Orkney Verse', *The Orkney Herald*, 26 June 1951.

— 'Reading Robert Rendall's Verse', *The Orcadian*, 24 September 1953.

— 'Robert Rendall's New Poems', *The Orkney Herald*, 8 October 1957.

— 'New Poems by the Orkney Laureate', *The Orcadian*, 20 October 1966.

Brown, John Flett and Murray, Brian, 'Dialect poems still strong after 40 years', *The Orcadian*, 14 June 2007.

Cursiter, Stanley, 'Robert Rendall's new book of Poems', *The Orcadian*, 3 October 1957.

Dickson, Neil T.R., *An Island Shore*, The Orkney Press (1990).

— 'God's Glory in Dandelions', *Third Way*, 14/2, March 1991.

— 'Littoral Truth: The Mind of Robert Rendall (1898–1967)', forthcoming.

Fergusson, James, Script for 'Arts Review' radio broadcast, BBC Scottish Home Service, 21 May 1947.

— 'A New Poet in Orkney', *The Glasgow Herald*, 29 May 1957.

Hall, Simon W., *The History of Orkney Literature*, Edinburgh, John Donald, 2010.

H[ewison], W[illiam], 'Robert Rendall's second book of verse', *The Orcadian*, 12 July 1951.

Lindsay, Maurice, *The Scottish Renaissance*, Edinburgh, Serif Books, 1948.

Linklater, Eric, 'The New Caledonians', *The Observer*, 8 February 1948.

Murray, Brian, 'Robert Rendall – a man of many talents', *The Orcadian*, 17 September 1998.

The Orcadian, 'Death of Robert Rendall Poet and Scholar', 15 June 1967.

— 'Letters Reveal Happy World of Robert Rendall', 9 May 1968.

Royle, Trevor, *A Time for Tyrants*, Edinburgh, Birlinn, 2011.

Young, Douglas, *"Plastic Scots" and the Scottish Literary Tradition*, MacLellan, Glasgow, 1948 ("Epitome of an address...on...22nd December, 1946").

Country Sonnets

& Other Poems

Dedicatory Verses

I sing the virtue
of country living,
Of long days spent
without misgiving,
In calm fulfilment
of rustic labours
Among good friends
and kindly neighbours.

I sing of Nature's
necromancy,
The beauty and wonder
that wake the fancy,
When after winter's
cheerless rigour
Gay summer flowers
the earth transfigure.

I sing of sea-swept
burial places,
Shore-graves where native
legend traces
Time's finger, and glimpses
as in vision
Our ancient Orkney
sea tradition.

Country Sonnets

The Shepherds

From Time's dim source still doth the music flow
    Of Hesiod's harp, in rustic measures bold,
    Lest, like a dream, the fabled age of gold
Should unrecalled from man's remembrance go.
On Virgil's plains we yet may soothe our woe,
    Watching the ploughman cleave the rich brown mould;
    Or Horace on his Sabine farm behold,
Leading afield his flock with flutings low.

High on the hillside, seated by their goats,
    Remain the shepherds, piping clear and strong
        Above the world's loud madness and its mirth.
Hark! Hear ye not these crownèd priests of song
    Sounding from age to age in deathless notes
        The immemorial wisdom of the earth?

Longing for a Country Life

Thrice ten reluctant years have I endured
    The tyranny of towns and shops and streets,
    Yet unsubdued my heart for freedom beats,
Not e'en by Time to servitude inured.
Ah no! The ancient passion is not cured,
    But wanders still in distant green retreats,
    Where the sown field with moorland pasture meets
And men move slow, of tranquil lives assured.

O for a quiet plot of fertile ground
    Whereon I might from civil cares exempt
    Peacefully labour. Wealth would never tempt
Me thence nor luxury, in cities found;
    But there should I, as oft in youth I dreamt,
Pass all my days, with rich contentment crowned.

Winter Mood

Day comes on silent foot, and earth awakes.
  Within their stackyards farmers come and go.
  In yonder field the ploughman, leaning low,
Furrow on furrow o'er the landscape makes.
He from the stillness of the morning takes
  A quiet mind, and motions calm and slow.
  Ah! Would that I with him might feel the flow
Of days and years beside these hills and lakes.

What wealth of inward joy and peace have they
  Who shepherd flocks or till the fruitful soil,
    Fulfilling 'neath the heav'ns' infinitude
Their daily task, nor wander far away;
  Each on his native croft content to toil,
    Season by season, matching Nature's mood.

Orkney Landscape

Such vistas have we here as oft exist
    When dreamy worlds bewitch our closing eyes;
    Far out before us in the distance lies
A sunny landscape steeped in golden mist.
The winding waters wander as they list
    Between green fields; along the hillside flies
    A shaft of sunlight, streaming down from skies
Of pearly cloud and purest amethyst.

Wide meadow-lands as these I've sometimes seen
    In ancient artistry. 'Tis thus portrayed:
    Within a spacious foreground sits a maid,
Beneath whose brows seraphic thoughts convene;
    While silver brooks, green swards, behind her fade,
Whence had been gained that sweet unruffled mien.

Birsay

Here on this rocky coast I roved, and here
    Beside the sea in happy boyhood played,
    Ere I had felt the bonds of ruthless trade
Or mourned time's loss through many a wasteful year.
Along these cliffs, when summer skies were clear,
    I watched the waves with thunder long delayed
    Break on the shore; or saw the colours fade
From evening clouds, and knew that night was near.

Here once again, where grow the wild sea-pinks,
    With idle steps I go, and mind at ease
From life's mad haste. O look! The red sun sinks
    In golden floods of light; and with the breeze
Comes faintly now across the grassy links
    The ageless music of the rolling seas.

Varro Dedicates His Book

I, Varro, baggage packed, would, ere I take
    My last farewell, and lie beneath the mould,
One parting gift to thee, Fundania, make:
    This little book that in my hand I hold.

'Twill make thee wise in ancient husbandries
    For thy new farm; teach management of herds,
Feeding of flocks, field-culture, care of bees;
    Rearing of goats and geese, snails, dormice, birds.

Days bring thought's full harvest, years fourscore
    Ripeness; and I, pondering how man may lead
The happy life, have gathered up this store
    Of rustic wisdom – a basket full of seed.

These grains of corn, riddled through Time's slow sieve,
May yet to thee life's richest increase give.

St. Gregory of Nazianzus Bids
Farewell to His Bishopric

Once more, farewell! I will not be denied
   Or hindered now. Nay, let another sit
   High on this mitred throne, for I shall quit
These worldly pomps and vanities. I'll ride
No more in gilded chariots, nor abide
   In princely courts, at tables exquisite
   Feasting long nights away, while wine and wit
Flow freely round to foster joyless pride.

In cloistered peace would I my days fulfil,
   And on sequestered fields, remote from strife,
     To lowly duties bend, though none applaud.
Elect ye then as bishop whom ye will!
   Give me my solitude, my country life,
     My quiet meditation, and my God.

Wide Waters

Wide waters! Such the prospect whence I take
   A sweet relief when overspent with care.
Beside the quiet margin of a lake
   Oft have I cooled my spirit, watching there

The ripples softly tinkling through the reeds,
   Whose thirsty roots stand sunk within the tide:
Or fair Apollo with his fiery steeds
   Behind the hills in golden splendour ride.

But when with long-sought leisure I at length
   Sit perched upon a rocky sea-swept height,
And view afar the slowly surging strength
   Of long Atlantic breakers, foaming white,

Before the flood of mighty seas my soul
Leaps in a tumult, answering roll for roll.

Siberian Spring

Suggested by a passage in Dostoievsky's 'House of the Dead'.

Compassionate Spring has set God's creatures free
    Who long have been in Winter's gloomy prison;
And out of dungeons dark how joyously
    The gentle flowers of the wood have risen.

April is come! And, lo, before her tabor
    As if by magic force each fetter breaks:
The mounting skylark makes the sun her neighbour,
    And every living thing its freedom takes.

Throughout the land, in valleys without number,
    The forest trees in fresh green leaf are found;
And shy small woodland beasts from winter slumber
    Creep forth to dance and sport upon the ground.

But shackled here 'mid shameful things and rotten
God's noblest work, sin-laden, lies forgotten.

Sonnets on Christian Faith

A Dedication

If with the magic of moonlight
    The heavens quicksilver the lake,
If from an archangel's pinion
    Droppeth the white snow-flake;
If beauty of light and shadow
    Be the fine art of the sun,
And if with threads ethereal
    The glorious rainbow is spun;
If from the clouds above us
    Are pools in the moorland filled,
If on the white narcissus
    The morning dew's distilled;
If by the breath of Heaven
    Earth lives, O then shall I
Sing songs in praise of my Maker,
    The Ruler of earth and sky.

David, the Shepherd

My flocks are in their fold, so now I keep
    A lonely vigil 'neath this mountain height.
    The silent beauty of the summer night
Awakes my fancy as I guard the sheep.
The earth, which throbs with life, although asleep,
    The glory of the skies in starry light,
    With equal voice declare their Maker's might
Till thought within me surges strong and deep.

What then is man that Thou should'st be so kind?
    Or what its worth that Thou dost love the world?
I looked to Thee with guilt-astonished mind
    For thunderbolts of justice to be hurled —
A Saviour comes! Now over me I find
    The glorious banner of Thy love unfurled.

St. Athanasius

He faced the world with noble reprimand,
    Raising a flinty bulwark 'gainst the shock
    Of Arian floods; himself a lofty rock,
Conspicuous 'mid the moving desert sand.
When ravening wolves beset the Libyan strand
    Under his shadow stood the witless flock
    Shielded and sheltered; while a stumbling-block
To foes was he, most formidably grand.

But storm-clouds came, and conflicts manifold;
    And o'er his head the wrath of hostile men
Like thunders of a mighty tempest rolled.
    Brave Athanasius! Didst thou meekly then
Remember Joseph by his brethren sold?
    Or Daniel walking in the lions' den?

A Prayer

How long, O Lord, must heavy skies and grey,
    Thick sunless clouds, and chilly glooms prevail,
    Before whose weight our wearied spirits fail,
Like parchèd flowers that wither and decay?
    For ever must we fretfully essay
    To pierce the heavens, and sadly thus bewail
    Our former courage? See how weak and frail
Thy creatures are, when mortal hopes betray.

Come with a cleansing if tempestuous wind,
    A sunny summer gale that swiftly drives
    The cheerless mists away. For joy revives
'Neath Thy blue firmament. Thus, though we've sinned,
    Be Thou our soul's bright health, so shall our lives
To stronger faith be duly disciplined.

Lyrics and Orkney Poems

The Praise of Beauty

O say not Beauty dies unsung.
    The passing cloud, the morning star,
The daffodil with dewdrops hung,
All lovely transient things and young
    Somewhere remembered are.

Shy violets were not born to wink
    'Neath dusky eyelids unadmired;
And grasses growing by the brink
Of moorland pools must each, I think,
    Have some fair song inspired.

It may be airy spirits haunt
    The woodland's unfrequented ways,
And where the blood-red poppies flaunt
In summer cornfields dryads chaunt
    Songs of immortal praise.

Though these be phantoms rarely seen
    'Tis fast within my bosom locked
That ne'er throughout this wide Demesne
Have ripened forms of wisdom been
    By dumb old Chaos mocked.

I will not heed your whisperings
    That Beauty's rapture may be crossed;
That, where she wanders, no one sings,
And that the loveliness of things
    Dies loverless and lost.

Beauty's Quest

O cloud! O winter Wind!
   Wand'ring across the skies.
In your lone flight I find
   An answer to my sighs.

O winter Wind and Cloud!
   Are ye, too, without rest?
By some wild impulse vowed
   To follow Beauty's quest?

O Cloud! O winter Wind!
   Knowing of my delight,
Will ye not henceforth bind
   My spirit with your flight?

Summer Flowers

See how the fields are overflowing
With sudden floods of summer flowers,
Trefoils and clovers spill their riches
Into the hollows and roadside ditches,
And buttercups in the meadows growing
Scatter like foam their golden showers.

The bright Sun stipples with hues entrancing,
Yellows and reds, unmixed, untainted,
Earth's brown canvas, and lightly sketches
Drifts of wild violets and purple vetches,
And poppies in the cornfields dancing —
As in a picture by Van Gogh painted.

Summer, the gipsy, now unfoldeth
Flowery meads, adroitly spreading
Fabrics, whose wealth of broidered stitches
So guilefully with beauty bewitches
As make the feet of him that beholdeth
Go dancing tiptoe, gay measures treading.

The Bargain

Now, in the early Spring,
    The wise old earth
Spends, in her bargaining,
    A golden sum
    Against the dearth
    Of days to come.

The crocuses unfold
    To the sun's rays
Their shining cloth of gold,
    To pay the debt
    Of sunny days
    Unseen as yet.

The yellow buttercup
    And pale cowslip
Are lightly lifted up
    Toward the blue,
    For the Sun to sip
    The morning dew.

And the marsh-marigold,
    By Spring restored,
Up from the winter mould
    Now brings to light
    A treasured hoard
    Of guineas bright.

O Summer sun to be,
    Shine out again!
Since NOW her words to thee
    The earth fulfils,
    Remember THEN
    The daffodils.

The Wooing of the Rose

Too rude was April's wooing —
   Alas, 'twas his undoing! —
Keen frost and fickle glances of the sun.
   A cold aloofness keeping,
The courtly Rose would not by him be won —
   And April went out weeping.

   But shyly May came wooing,
   Love tremblingly pursuing:
He peeped out from behind a little cloud.
   A thrush her song was voicing.
In maiden green the Rose her love avowed —
   And May came in rejoicing.

Winter

Winter that waketh
    The storm on the seas,
Bendeth and breaketh
The strong bough and shaketh
    The roots of the trees,
Moves on my spirit
    As upon these.

Winter, the giant,
    Has wrathfully hurled
A challenge defiant
Against a too pliant
    And sensuous world:
The heavy cloud-banners
    Are darkly unfurled.

Shivering hedges
    Are stripped by his breath;
Tall, withered sedges
By lonely lake edges
    Are frozen in death —
Winter is scornful
    What anyone saith.

Flower Ghosts

The green leaves and blossoms wither,
    And falling one by one are sown
    In the brown earth, or else blown,
By the wind's breath, hither and thither.

I walk now in the winter garden
    Down the path where the ghosts go
    Of dead flowers, mourning the woe
Of the fair forms they once were starred in.

A disembodied pink pentstemon
    By the far trellis fans its wings,
    And hereabout are found the things
Spirits of drooping poppies dream on.

Troops of pale shadows lightly flicker
    Where once the tall sweet-Williams were,
    And at my footfall, I aver,
Trip to and fro with dancings quicker.

A faint fragrance of unseen roses
    Comes to me like the breath of June,
    From where, in its appointed noon,
The sweetest summer wind that blows is.

When Spring comes, and I am working
    In the warm mould, will these escape
    To the sun's height, or here take shape
The while in fragrant corners lurking?

I only know, 'tis man's first duty
    In old gardens and woodland shades
    To walk softly the dim glades
So heavily haunted with vanished beauty.

The Night Wind

A wind wandered in from the sea,
    A wind forlorn, unexpected,
    But with deep-sea music and magic infected
The wanderer visited me.

Deep in the dead of the night,
    When men and cattle were sleeping,
    Up through the valley the wet wind came creeping
With tremulous footsteps and light.

A lonely ghost of the seas,
    An outcast unwelcomed, unwanted,
    That whistled and moaned as it drearily haunted
The tops of the shivering trees.

A wind wandered in from the sea,
    A wind forlorn, unexpected,
    But with deep-sea music and magic infected
The wanderer visited me.

Orkney

God, Who in days of old
    Created the sea
And the skies – O there behold
    What beauties be —
These treeless islands set
    Where the wild-goose flies,
Lest men should e'er forget
    The sea and the skies.

In a Churchyard

I, who beside this trim
    Green churchyard plot,
Downbending, think of him
    Who now is not,
Wonder if sometimes he
    On the clouds that pass
Looks down (rememb'ring me)
    As I on the grass.

The Fisherman

Adapted from Andrew Lang's Translation of Leonidas of Tarentum.

Aald Jeems o' Quoys, wha erst wi' leid and line
    Keen as a whitemaa, reaped the Rousay Soond,
And in his weathered yawl a twalmonth syne
    Set lapster-creels the Westness craigs aroond,
Nae stroke o' fortune cloured wi' bluidy claa,
    Nor glow'ring daith wi' sudden tempest mocked,
But in his wee thatched croft he wore awa'
    E'en as a cruisie flickers oot unslockt.
Nae kinsman raised, nor wife, nor weeping w'ain,
    But we, his yamils, this memorial stane.

Orkney Crofter

Scant are the few green acres that I till,
But arched above them spreads the boundless sky,
   Ripening their crops; and round them lie
      Long miles of moorland hill.

Beyond the cliff-top glimmers in the sun
The far horizon's bright infinity;
   And I can gaze across the sea
      When my day's work is done.

The solitudes of land and sea assuage
My quenchless thirst for freedom unconfined;
   With independent heart and mind
      Hold I my heritage.

The Town

From the German of Theodor Storm.

A dim grey strand, a dim grey sea,
　　And nearby lies the town.
Mist hangs on roof-tops heavily,
And through the stillness sounds the sea
　　With sad note o'er the town.

No rustling woods in summer's height,
　　Nor small birds, cheer the land.
The wild-goose through the harvest night
With harsh voice screaming takes its flight;
　　Shore-grasses fluttering stand.

Yet clings my whole heart still to thee,
　　Thou grey town by the tide.
The charm of youth eternally
Lies smiling still on thee, on thee,
　　Thou grey town by the tide.

A Country Burial

A stranger in the parish,
      I followed with the farm-folk
The upward-winding track
      between the winter fields,
And upon the hill-top
      stood among the mourners
Round the open grave
      in the still church-yard.

Distantly I heard
      the old prayer intoned,
Committing dust to dust,
      the soul to God Who gave,
But e'er a clod could fall
      in the grass-strewn grave
A sudden lark arose
      with a loud burst of singing.

I alone, enraptured,
      saw the mounting bird
As if it were a spirit
      through the far clouds winging.

Kirkyard by the Shore

In this old kirkyard lay my coffined bones,
      That I, perchance, like those within these graves,
      On winter nights may hear the waves
      Thundering among the stones.

The Spell

On all four corners of her neighbour's field
      She places egg-shells, filled with golden butter.
      "Thistles," hear the old witch mutter,
      "This ground shall henceforth yield"

The Knowe

Wrecked on the ocean wave were we
    Who late were cast upon the shore,
Whence to this knowe beside the sea
    Sea-faring men our bodies bore.
But here though lodged among the dead,
    We oft, when evening falls, can feel
The laden fisher homeward tread
    With basket filled from line and creel.

Cliff Grave, Hoy

We found them at the break of day,
  Prostrate, and cold, and stiff—
Two miners locked in deadly fray
  Beside the moorland cliff.

In one rude grave we laid the twain;
  Then walled the plot around,
Lest wandering cattle should profane
  Their lonely burial ground.

Town-Dwellers

Flies, buzzing upon the window-pane,
Beating wings vainly against invisible glass;
Light-loving,
And feeling the urge of free inconsequent flight.

Struck by a child's hand into sudden death,
Or ash-bucketed with table scraps and sweepings;
Mere dust,
Fly-papered as a nuisance in the house.

What else are we, droning rhythmic measures
Against incomprehensible ceilings,
Winged dreamers,
Of Time's infinitude conscious and fathomless space?

Tailpiece

Scarabrae Re-Visited

Young fools may scoff, and wise men sneer
At curious facts recorded here.
Tuts! Let them die, who with clipped wings
Outlive the magic heart of things,
And flutter up and down with moans
On hard commercial paving-stones.
But I, I like to think a street
Retains the touch of buried feet,
That window panes in shops remember
Festivities of last December,
That unsuspected walking-sticks
Are haunted by their masters' tricks,
And that some social virtue lingers
In tea-cups held by human fingers,
That epicureans' wisest thoughts
Are chronicled in old jam-pots.

Be these surmises as they may,
I one time went to Scarabrae
To view with antiquarian dream
The prehistoric housing scheme.
Alas for thoughts of old romance!
I found myself, by merest chance,
Preceded by a picnic party
Of flesh and blood, whose hale and hearty
Voices split in sweet confusion
The spectacles of my illusion.

I nodded, inwardly most furious,
To groups of youthful blades and curious
And mused why girls with bobbed hair

Should crowd a Pictish thoroughfare.
Plainly, the thing was past a joke,
For everybody laughed or spoke,
The accents of a genial parson
Urbanely leading this vain farce on.
Old broken bones from family cloisters,
Deer's antlers, perforated oysters,
Were scattered round, or else were thrown
(With half-suspected bits of stone)
By masons' shovels into sacks —
For this we must pay income-tax!

But as I wandered, much dejected,
Throughout the village re-erected,
I found a fragment, somewhat lipped,
Of ancient china, badly chipped.
"Ah!" murmured I (without humbug),
"A prehistoric shaving-mug!"
'Twas used, perchance, there is no knowing,
In that first early hirsute mowing
Which Pictish youths – 'tis said – grew rash on
When mutton-chops went out of fashion.
I – absent-minded – rubbed the rim
Till magic made the daylight dim.

Strange darkness fell, the very cleric
Vanished in thin blue atmospheric
Mist, and all the party mostly
Turned little wisp-like forms and ghostly,
Which came and went with flickering stirs
As ancient Pictish villagers.

The man in black emerged anew
A solid Pictish man in blue,
Who at the gate with smile seraphic,
And beckoning thumb, controlled the traffic.

These tribal building innovations
Breed municipal regulations
Whose brief importance, more or less,
Denote a civic consciousness.
The law had come, with slow defenders
'Gainst loungers, barrows, limpet vendors,
And all in Scara's highways hawking
Heard some fat voice say, "Keep on walking."

Awhile between the crooked winding
Walls I wandered, ever finding
Bits of re-enacted history
(Let him who can explain the mystery).
I peered through passages whose headroom
Was scant enough, and saw a bedroom
Where one old village patriarch
Lay chewing limpets in the dark.

A small salt well was by his bedstead,
And crones, with shakings of the head, said
He took, despite much village scorning,
His breakfast in his bed each morning.
There was no need for him to scrimp it:
He just reached down and took a limpet.

Of trading guilds, whose merchants sought
My custom for the things they wrought,
Flint-workers, mussel-pudding bakers,
Stone-hammer smiths, bone-needle makers,
I must pass by nor give exciting
Records of the runic writing:
Whoso would relish more, indeed,
Must, I assure them, merely read,
With sentimental eyes tear-pearled,
Back numbers of the Scara Herald.

Orkney Variants

& Other Poems

Dedicatory Verses to Miss Janet Couper

BY WHOSE FRIENDSHIP
I HAVE BEEN HONOURED SINCE BOYHOOD

Old happy times in Birsay spent
Come back to fill me with content.
Two brothers were we: in our play
As boys we lived but by the day,
Beneath a wise maternal eye
Learning the charms of sea and sky,
Until the sun sank, flaming red,
Between the Brough and Marwick Head.
But did we late or early roam,
Your little cottage was our home.
We poked about in ebb-tide holes
To fill with crabs your pudding bowls,
And many an evening, from the shore
Spread whelks and starfish on your floor.

I brought you, too, with youthful shout
My first proud catch of Birsay trout.
There, at the burn where long ago
I watched the water seaward flow
Bearing our treasured small cork boats
Rigged with hen-feathers, ever floats
A mimic fleet from seggies made
By two small boys that loved to wade,
Barefooted, in those shallow spots
Where grew the bright forget-me-nots:
I yet can of an evening feel
That long slow draw of fast-hooked eel.

When tides were low we sought to reach
Our Crusoe island on the beach,
Or with the herd-boy on the links
Sat down among the wild sea-pinks.
But when I think of those oat-cakes
And scrumptious puddings and home-bakes
With which your kind hand, noon and night,
Regaled our boyish appetite...
Though feasted since, I still prefer
To think how fortunate we were.

For all our ploys and simple sport
The summer days proved all too short;
And, as boys will, who cannot sleep
When nights are fine, but softly creep
Out through ben windows, so we went,
And ranged your garden in content,
Well pleased to think that no one knew
What steerie boys had planned to do.
(Though once it chanced, by perverse luck,
This truant in the window stuck!)

How pleasant were those Sabbath days,
Long gone, when we walked up the braes,
And in the Kirk-abune-the-hill
Sat with you, keeping hushed and still,
And from your loft-pew, looking down,
Watched the precentor's shining crown.
If from remembered joys like these
Poets derive their power to please,
If by such friendliness alone
As I down at the Place have known
Man's inward happiness endures,
Then, Janet, this small book is yours.

To the Compositors and Printers of this Book

Quick! Here is a handful of birds,
   fluttering, only half-caught.
Snare them in a cage of words,
   these swift migrants of thought.

They have wings – hold them fast,
   even though they screech!
Huddle them into type, but cast
   a separate page for each...

Orkney linticks, singing, perchance,
   a brief summer song;
Slow, sad ravens that dance
   with rhythmic steps along;

House-sparrows, friendly to man,
   chirruping as they hop;
Chattering starlings, eager to scan
   Kirkwall from the chimney-top;

And, it may be, a chance nightingale,
   winged with Aegean rhyme,
Teaching our island groves a tale
   still fresh and old as Time...

Yours be it on the printed page
   to prison them in the North:
Others will open the cage,
   and see the birds fly forth.

Poems in Dialect

Cragsman's Widow

"He was aye vaigan b' the shore,
    An' climman amang the craigs,
Swappan the mallimaks,
    Or taakan whitemaa aiggs.

"It's six year bye come Lammas,
    Sin' he gaed afore the face,
An' nane but an aald dune wife
    Was left tae work the place.

"Yet the sun shines doun on a' thing,
    The links are bonnie and green,
An' the sea keeps ebban an' flowan
    As though it had never been."

By wi' the Sea

Owre fail'd tae rive in face o' angry seas
Or sit apae a thaft and lift an oar,
A'm dune wi' sea-wark. I maun bide ashore,
Bitin' me thoom, while ithers catch the breeze.
But though me joints are aald and growan stiff,
I'll bigg apae the green a steethe o' stanes,
And whummle than on tap me tarry skiff
Tae sair for shelter tae a dizzen hens.
Baith man and boat, mebbe, in spite o' weather
For twa'rthree winters yet'll haad together.

Salt i' the Bluid

A'm bydan heem, 'at geed for lang
  Ruggan afore the mast,
Yet times me thowts they taak a spang
  Aff tae the wild Nor'wast.

On winter nights I whiles can feel
  Me cottage gaan adrift,
An' wance again I grip the wheel
  Tae the sea-swaal's aisy lift.

Whan lood swaps gouster at the door,
  An' the nort' wind tirls the sneck,
Full canvas on, we drive afore,
  As whaalbacks sweep the deck.

Spier no for siklike ferlies proof!
  Things chance when nights are lang:
The very timmers o' the roof
  Creak as we dunt alang.

The Planticru

Whaur green abune the banks the links stretch oot
    On tae the sandy noust, lies midway there
An aald-time planticru, smothered aboot
    In weeds – but fu' weel delled, and dressed wi' ware.
Biggid o' sea-worn boolders fae the beach
    A dyke runs roond it, lichened doun the sides,
Scarce keepan leaf and root beyond the reach
    O' winter gales and fierce Atlantic tides.

'Oors lang, an age-bent wife wi' aspect mild
    Stands gazan oot tae sea; or digs a speel,
Slowly, as if by vagrant thowts beguiled,
    And sets her twa'rthree tatties i' the dreel;
Nor kens hoo firm she haads b' siklike toil
Man's aald inheritance o' sea and soil.

I' the Kirk Laft

Here i' the sooth laft's neuks sae dim,
Twa aald-time relics – Haad thee wits!
A hangman's ladder twa could clim',
A widden pulpit, geen tae bits.

Whaur ither should they than in kirk
O' guid and evil mind us a'.
Time plays, hooever, mony a quirk:
Prelate and tief are baith awa.

Mansie's Threshing

The mune was up, and the starnie lift
    Luk'd doun wi' an eerisome licht,
As Mansie ap-raise fae his neuk-bed
    In the wee sma 'oors o' the nicht.
      Green O green grew the corn.

The Lady's Elwand was high in the aist
    Wi' mony anither starn,
When Mansie ap-raise fae his neuk-bed,
    And syne gaed through tae the barn.
      Green O green grew the corn.

He saa the mune-beams glint on the wa'
    Lik' spooks on kirk-yaird graves,
As doun fae the twart-backs he tuk' the flail
    Tae thresh oot his load o' shaeves.
      O bonnie and green grew the corn.

He grippid a shaef, he rissl'd the heid,
    He cuist it apae the floor.
"Trow tak me," he said, "if shaeves lik' this
    Were seen on the place afore."
      Green O green grew the corn.

"The neebors minted what nane wad neem
    When the knowe cam' under the pleugh;
But heth, the stooks were cairted heem,
    And biggid a denty skroo."
      Green O green grew the corn.

"Wha meddle wi' Pickie-knowes, said they,
     Ill-skaith wad them befa' —
But never a ferlie cam' near me,
     Nor ever a thing ava."
          O green grew the corn on the knowe.

The soople, swung abune his heid,
     Had twirled but three times three,
When Mansie afore him b' the wa'
     An aasome sight did see.
          Green O green grew the corn.

A black-haired bockie, wi een that lowed
     Lik' the flame in a howkit neep,
A faersomlik' mooth wi' a yellow tooth,
     And lugs that hung in a fleep.
          O bonnie and green grew the corn.

It glowered and gloomed, till the haet haet bluid
     Louped fast in Mansie's veins,
For the bockie's flail, baith soople and staff,
     Wis a deid man's white shank-banes.
          O green on the knowe grew the corn.

Then up spak Mansie and stootly said,
     "A'm blide o' thee company,
But bees' thoo Pight, or barrow-wight,
     Come thresh fornent o' me."
          O bonnie and green grew the corn.

"For the baists maun be fed, and the windlins spread,
  Though the world be fu' o' spooks,
The corn be mill'd, and the girnel fill'd
  Wi' bere fae the guid corn-stooks."
    Green, green grew the corn on the knowe.

Aa' through the barn the mettins spret
  Lik' sparks fae a smiddy fire,
And aye the stour the thicker cam'
  And the haeps o' strae raise higher.
    Green O green grew the corn.

Faster and fiercer fell the flails,
  Till the mune cam' roond on the wa',
And the cruisie flickered, and gaed clean oot,
  And they heard the reid cock craa.
    Green O green grew the corn.

Hoo it befell, O nane can tell,
  But when they brak doon the door,
Wi' bluid on his heid, they fand him deid
  On an empty threshing floor.
    O green grew the corn on the knowe.

They laid him in the green kirk-yaird,
  But for midnights three times three,
They heard deep doun in the hert o' the knowe
  The soond o' revelrie.
    Green O green grew the corn.

  "Green O green grew the corn,
  Bonnie and green grew the corn,
  Green on the knowe grew the corn—O
  Bonnie and green grew the corn."

Shore Tullye

An experiment in Scaldic metre

Crofters few but crafty,
Krugglan doun b' moonlight,
Hidan near the headland,
Hint great congles waited.
Swiftly rude sea-raiders
Stranded, evil-handed:
Scythe blades soon were bleedan,
Skulls crackt in the tullye.

Stretched the battle beachward;
Bravely back we drave them.
Een fleep fleean hinmost
Fand we maakan landward:
Him apae the hillside
Hewed we doun in feud fight —
Never kam sea-rovers
Seekan back tae Rackwick.

Orkney Variants

On Reading Some Translations
from the Greek Anthology

These are our own, the songs of ancient Greece,
The island songs that sing of sea and soil
And days of unremitting toil
Crown'd with idyllic peace.

Whether in far Tarentum found, or leas
Sicilian, keep they still the fluted note
Caught from enchanting sounds that float
From distant Aegean seas.

Sing them, for still in Rousay and in Wyre
On little crofts where fragrant peat yet burns,
Alone, old Platthis sits and turns
Her wheel beside the fire.

Leonidas, with piping finger, charms
Our ears, as on our island roads we walk,
Watching with him plain country folk
On Orkney's hillside farms.

The rude sea-faring men whose weathered bones,
Nameless, lie buried where the salt spray blows
On Rackwick's grassy knowes, are those
Crinagoras bemoans.

Hushed flocks that once, bemused, heard Bion strike
His Lydian chords – these, too, are with us still,
And meekly browse upon the hill
Beside the Binscarth dyke...

Launch them upon our native dialect,
New-rigged in Viking fashion, tight and trim;
Nor let one single song on grim
Oblivion's reef be wrecked.

Celestial Kinsmen

After Marcus Argentarius

The winter lift is glintan doun
Wi' tullimentan stars besprent,
As were the very heavens abune
Clean gyte wi' frosty merriment,
Their lowan e'en are taakan tent
O' chiels like Mansie o' the Bu'
Whase days upon the land are spent
Ruggan wi' Taurus and the Pleugh.

Contentment

After Leonidas of Tarentum

Look! This is Liza's but and ben,
Wi' screen o' bourtrees tae the door,
Her stack o' peats, her flag-roofed byre,
Her planticru abune the shore;
Yet 'mang her hens and hoosehold gear
She's bruck'd aboot for eighty year.

Doun at the P'lace

After Antiphilus of Byzantium

If aa' were as I would, and fate were kind, I'd hae the gift
O' vaigan roond wi' Jeems alang the tide-mark gathering
drift,
I would on summer mornings, aff Skaehua, haal the creels,
Or fish for lythe; whiles taak the oars a bit, in easy speels:
And, evening come, I'd maak oot by the Brough in Willie's
boat,
As I sae aft hae deun, lang syne, content tae be afloat:
Or as the streen, wi' some aald fisher stand, and fae a rock
Catch a few cuithes – for I hae aye been blyde o' ord'nar'
folk.

Haad Aff, Haad Aff the Pleugh

After Heraclitus

Haad aff, haad aff the pleugh, nor saa thee seed
Here b' the knowe, whaur sleep the ancient deid,
Aald banes hae po'er o' ill, and fegs, it's true,
That if thoo disna heed
The Pights 'll maak thee grue.
Haad aff, haad aff the pleugh!

Envy

After Lucilius

Young Magnus wi' the muckle teeth
           For very madrum's deid:
His brither sheep-thief dirls beneath
           A higher gallows-heid.

Plain Fare: Guid Lear

After Lucian

Hibernicus aye scowlds the lass wha bakes
Sweet savouries, merangues, and pasty cakes,
And scunnert, flytes, "Bold huzzy, wouldst thou dare
Tae meddle wi' a Scotsman's honest fare?"
Yet when o' oatmeal brose he's cleaned the plate
Tae glaip some venison he's naething blate,
And woodcock pie goes weel, it's finely kent,
Wi' frugal meals and soond Scots' argument.

The Happy Isle

After Detlev von Liliencron

The ulie-lamp reeks in the muify byre,
Whaur, ooran wi' content, twa nowt lie spraalan:
Rooster and hens claa tight apae the hallan,
Scrattan in gloondie dreams amang the mire.
The crofter's laddie wi' his shepherd's reed
Aald-farrant tunes plays tae his peerie brither,
And bairns and kye and birds aa' thirled together
Let this world's tide gang swirlan ower their heid.

The Twa

After Hugo von Hofmannsthal

Wi' danglan shanks and tousled hair
And whistlan owre a country tune
Intae the yard he rode the mare,
Cried, "Whoa," and louped fu' lightly doun.

She cam' oot fae the byre door
Wi' milk pails sweeman tae the brim,
And stepp'd alang sae douce and prim
A single drap ne'er lippid owre.

Yet when the lad in ilka hand
The weel-filled buckets fain wad tak,
Ere ane the tither's fingers fand
(Sae potent was their saft desire)
The twa at aince began tae shak;
And guid white milk ran doun the syre.

Hinmost Days

After Richard von Schaukal

The aald man still keeps wand'ran
       Tae the brecks besooth the yaird:
He's naething noo tae lippen,
       He's by wi' it aa', he's faer'd.

Wi' fing'rs cruikit and bluidless
       He grips the heids o' corn:
He kens it's weel nigh deun wi'
       Yet bides as he wis born.

Poems in English

Winter Threshing

As within a dream,
Dim shapes flicker and fall
On the gable wall:
Spectral shadows flung
By the lantern hung
'Neath the loft's low beam.

From the mill's great mouth
Comes, with deepening wails,
Gust on windy gust,
Like autumnal gales
Whirling high the dust
After summer's drouth.

Now the golden grain
Falls like April rain:
Chaff, like floating mist
By the sunshine kisst,
Brings again the dawn
Of May-mornings gone.

Idly drifting by
To the roof's dim span,
Straw-clouds come and go:
In the barn below,
Ghostlike, moves a man,
Raking down the sky.

'Mid the winter storms,
Viewless, voiceless forms,
Bound by Nature's chain
To the circling year,
Dance in solemn train
Round Earth's mystic sphere.

In procession slow
Grave immortals go.
Move the seasons four,
As in days of yore,
With Pandean song,
Hand in hand, along.

Still upon the wall
Dim shapes flicker and fall:
Swift light-footed fauns,
Seen again in trance
In their ritual dance
On Hellenic lawns.

The Orkney Primula

"Primula Scotica"
Though they have named thee,
Thou art of Norway
    Far over the foam,
And in the ancient
Isles of the Earldom,
Primrose of Orkney,
    Makest thy home.

Blooming in exile
Far from thy homeland,
Starring with beauty
    The sea-scented turf,
Daylong like distant
Music thou hearest
Sagas Norwegian
    Sung by the surf.

Not on the corn-clad
Fields of the Mainland
Mapped out and measured
    According to plan,
Nor on their cattle-filled
Meadows or ploughlands
Thriv'st thou in pastures
    Trodden by man;

But where the thundering
Waves of the ocean
Echo the war-cry
    Of Einar and Sweyn,
High on the cliff-top
Spell-bound thou standest,
Silently dreaming
    Of Thorfinn's domain.

Haunting the headlands
And sea-links of Westray,
Perched on the cliff-tops
    Of Sandwick and Skaill,
Dost thou in daydreams
Glimpse, as in old times,
Dragon-prowed vessels
    Voyaging sail?

Still on the mind's high
Clifflands surviving
Blossom the glories
    Of Rognvald's great name;
Still do the silent
Hearts of the Northmen
Proudly remember
    Magnus' bright fame.

Primrose of Orkney!
From the great sea-cliffs
Far o'er the islands
    Scatter thy seed,
Bid thou awaken
Men like the Vikings,
Mighty in singing
    And doughty in deed.

The Kelp-Worker

I walked, a bygone summer day,
The sandy links of a sea-blown bay.

And there an old kelp-worker met,
Whose lone gaunt figure haunts me yet.

His hands, heaven's gift for daily needs,
Were gnarled like withered tangle-weeds.

The gentle strength of summer skies,
Long looked at, filled the old man's eyes.

He moved about upon the beach,
Wary of step and scant of speech,

And wore with aspect of renown
The beauty that is labour's crown.

Erling's Rune

'Neath the low lintel
Of Maeshowe's tomb,
   Like others led,
Thou, too, Ingiborg
The fair widow
   Bowed thy head.

Many a high lady
Haughty and proud
   Has entered before thee.
Ah, Ingiborg,
In the darkness thou liest,
   And none to adore thee.

King Hakon's Dirge

Ye waves that meet
Where strong tides surge,
Go wail the dirge
Of proud defeat
O'er Hakon's fleet.

Ships full six-score
At anchor lay.
War-shields they bore
In ranked array,
And banners gay.

Death comes, alas,
On raven wings,
And even kings
Like shadows pass
From mortal things.

The sun's eclipse
With sudden gloom
And pallid lips
Foretold the doom
Of these fair ships.

Ye waves that meet
Where strong tides surge,
Again repeat
Grief's wail, and beat
King Hakon's dirge.

The Moorland Cottage

Idling I went where moorland heights
    Were warm with summer's breath,
But in the midst of my delights
    I saw the print of death:

A hillside cottage, left of yore
    Untenanted and lone,
With crazy windows cobwebbed o'er,
    And walls of crumbling stone.

Around the house like still soft rain
    An eerie silence lay,
As if its living soul had ta'en
    A voyage worlds away.

The Horse-Mill

Beside the heavenly meadows daisied with stars
The planets yoked in team – Uranus, Mars,
Jove, Neptune, Venus, Mercury, Saturn, Earth —
Not saddled now to run with tightened girth,
But to the mill's unwieldy lever bound,
Wheel their enormous burden round and round.
Linked to the trees, harnessed with hame and trace,
They stumble round the tracks of cosmic space,
With slow hard step, necks bent, and flanks a-sweat
Turning yon beam, the sun for axle set.
To grind what corn in what celestial mill
Move these great Titans, shouldering onward still?

Museum Piece

I've got the butterfly pinned on the cork!
Here it is – a poem, that only two days ago
Like a leaf, flew upward in wild abandon
Along invisible lanes of light.

See! It still flutters, quivering,
Impatient again on intangible wings
To explore, with quick sentient antennae,
Fathomless deeps in the upper air.

Look how its wings with hieroglyphics —
Alpha, upsilon, sigma, tau —
Deftly arranged in rhyme and rhythm
Stammer with beauty that dies in speech.

For even as with breathless wonder
I trace its markings, doubt creeps in:
Since, seen in flight, its painted splendour
Was a flash of colour lost in light.

In the moment of triumph when thought's swift net
The living flame of spirit ensnared,
And held its luminous wings in check
(But brushing off their powdered beauty),

Ah – whither went that ecstasy of delight,
That madness, dissolving into the sun,
That radiance, bright with transparency of joy,
That primal freedom, evoking flight?

Of all that animate essence – butterfly
Or poem – what have I now to show you?
Only this frail anatomy of words,
Dusted over with the legacy of death.

Vigil

After the German of Rainer Maria Rilke

Dim fields are sleeping now,
My heart keeps watch alone;
Evening, in harbour now,
Her red sail furls anon.

Dream vigil! Now the night
Goes pacing through the land;
The moon, a lily white,
Blossoms within her hand.

Flight Home

Lost in the clouds and anchorless in space,
    I think of those charmed islands whence I came,
Whither I now return – the one fixed place
    Where life's calm happiness remains the same.
From other lands, from other seas and skies
    Where I of late have been so strangely hurled,
A thousand images before me rise
    Like shadows of an insubstantial world.
Sunny Italian courtyards, Alpine snow,
    Peasants upon the fields, loud mountain streams,
Cities of marbled splendour found where flow
    Arno and Tiber, melt again to dreams:
For suddenly all Orkney comes in sight
And I look down to hail it with delight.

Orkney Summer

A timeless beauty breaks on loch and hill,
    As did the sun, in his diurnal flight,
    Stay, at high noon, his golden chariot bright,
And all the summer fields with radiance fill.
Those moorland brecks, these meadows by the mill,
    And valleys green, tremulous with delight,
    Lie lapped in vapours luminous and white:
The very clouds hang motionless and still.

Such beauty yet has power to tranquilize
    Earth's ancient discord. Once again is found
Saturnian peace; and here, 'neath Orkney skies
    Lone man, the immortal dreamer, dimly sees,
Beyond Time's change and Ocean's utmost bound
    The islands of the lost Hesperides.

Open Atlantic, Birsay

Kings here nor heroes proud advantage hold:
 Time's wave obliterates their bannered fame,
 Wrecked upon memory's reef. Even Magnus' name
Haunts, tombless, this green churchyard, unextolled;
And native histories, burnished once like gold,
 Reft from men's minds, are gone without reclaim.
 Here Nature ruled long ere the Northmen came,
And wrinkled waves against these headlands rolled.

Wild oracles, with measured ebb and flow,
 Beat, day and night, upon this lonely beach,
  And I again can hear with sudden thrill
Tides that return from timeless years ago
 With syllables of unremembered speech,
  That in the mind's deep silence echo still.

The Orkney Earls

Scorning beneath ignoble servitude
    To bow their necks, where they had lived at ease,
    They launched their ships upon the western seas,
And, dauntless, matched their fate, as brave men should.
Thence came the race whose island earls subdued
    The Pictish tribes, made Dalriadic leas
    Ring with their swords, and through the Hebrides
Swept forward in proud conquest unwithstood.

But greater omens in the North appeared,
    When thick and green sprang up the virgin grass
        Where Magnus fell, when hands with skill devout
This old red minster, stone by stone, upreared,
    And the far Mediterranean heard the shout
        Of Rognvald's men, and saw their longboats pass.

Lord of Time

I saw the cities falling one by one
   Whose stones were built in blood, by tyrants' hire:
   Thebes and Nineveh, Rome, Athens, Tyre,
And by the great Euphrates, Babylon.
As forests kindled by the flaming sun,
   Red on the sky-line, so, a funeral pyre
   Far off, the nations melted, heaped in fire,
Shattered by atom-bomb and rocket-gun.

I watched their smoke's black furnace wreathing climb
   Up through the heavens, when lo, like oriflamme
     The clouds unrolled, and a loud trumpet pealed,
     As came in view a Throne, all chariot-wheeled
   And ringed in light, and on the throne a Lamb,
Down-riding to restore the wastes of time.

The Transfiguration

Climbing steep slopes, with Peter, James and John,
   He made ascent of Hermon's cloudy height
   – Heaven's Lord, whom once the angels bore in flight –
When, lo, His face with sudden radiance shone,
More glorious than the sun to look upon;
   And all His holy garments, glittering white,
   Flashed, as no crystal jewels can make bright,
Nor fuller's art hold in comparison.

Robed heralds, also, in attendance due
   Stood near their King, and His high Paschal named.
This service given, Elias went from view
   As one forgotten; Moses' form grew dim:
And from the Cloud a trumpet-voice proclaimed,
   "This is My Son, My Chosen, hear ye Him!"

Tailpiece

Lament for the Legends

Sin' I hed little o' the schule
Yin toonsfolk traet me lik' a fule
   Meed but tae tak the len' o'.
Them! Let them golder as they will
For heth, there's things ahint the hill
   Yin learn'd folk little ken o'.
They hinno seen the muckle tyke
    'At fleggid Willie Chalmers,
Or h'ard oot b' the aald hill-dyke
    The trolls 'at ha'nt the hammers
      Start gowlan and howlan
    Until the white-faced moon,
      Sair plaguid, grows fleggid,
    An' than gings skrinklan doun.

Wha disna ken witch-fires are seen
Lowan aa' night each Hallowe'en
   Apae the hill o' Ravie?
Or niver h'ard hoo witless folk
Lang bydan on an ebb-tide rock
   Were teen b' Nuckelavee?
Whase skinless limbs an' fiery braeth
    An' whaals-mooth maist undaemin
Wad fleg a mortal clean tae daeth:
    His reid eye fixed an' flaman
      Fair quell'd them, an' held them,
    Until his faersome claas
      Hed touch'd them an' clutch'd them —
    As wis wi' Rab o' Flaws.

Sea-gaan is no whit wance it wis,
For gey unchancy wark tuk pläce
   Afore they hed the sprole.
I mind oot b' the Evie shore
Hoo treeskie Fin-folk gripp'd an oar
   An' weel-nigh couped the yole.
An' maist o' times ill-veekit trows
   Their Tangie-tricks wad try,
Wad yirk awa the huicks, an' lowse
   The aethic-stane forby,
     Till ruggan an' tuggan
   Near aa' the fish were teen,
     Or nippid an' grippid
   They wirno wort' a preen.

Wha noo hes sight o', tell thoo me,
Eynhallow glaiped ap b' the sea
   In glamsy blinks o' weather?
Or watched young selkies at their play
On lang-lost cletts o' rock apae
   The shores o' Heather-blether?
Though green holms, steeped in summer haze,
   Forget their common birth,
An' lie enchanted clean for days
   Afloat apae the firth.
     They glimmer an' shimmer
   Atween the sea an' sky,
     Times driftan or shiftan,
   Whiles vanishing forby.

The north isles steamer maaks her roond
By Eday Pier an' Stronsay Soond;
    She lands the mails at Papey.
The soothboat wi' her mastheid lights
Glides doun the String on Friday nights,
    The Ola sails b' Scapey.
But wha hes iver wance teen trip
    Fae Westray or the toun
In Orkney's muckle Mester-ship,
    Whase foretop rakes the moon?
        Though whiles, min, an islesman,
    Divertan wi' the boys,
        Tae flix them, fair tricks them
    Wi' tales o' siclike ploys.

The islands rax their aald rock-banes,
The flude o' summer fills their veins,
    Aesan the pains o' winter.
The moorland brecks are bright wi' floo'rs,
The larks are singan at aa' 'oors,
    An' Life casts care ahint 'er.
But luik ye, niver noo in Vore
Can man hear tell o' Terran,
Rampagan on the ocean floor,
    For folk are little carean
        Hoo tullyas or brullyas
    Fought wi' the great Sea-mither
        B' swordship gae lordship
    Tae ane or else the tither.

A'm ha'rd them neem whin I wis young
The Stoor-worm wi' his forkie tongue.
   Faith, some aald folk hed spied it!
Seven maidens glaiped he in a week,
Or fairly mad, meed sic a reek
   Nae mortal sowl could bide it.
For there he wis at break o' dawn
   Whin Saturday cam' roond,
An' t'ree times t'ree gaed sic a yawn
   The weeman-folk aa' swooned.
     Tae taak them and brak them
     Atween his muckle teeth
      The deemon cam' sweeman
     An' drew them underneath.

Than Assipattle i' his boat
Gaed scullan doun the monster's thro't:
   The lik' o't did thoo iver!
Till swallowed lik' a bit o' maet
He ap an' wi' a reid-hot paet
   Set fire t' Stoor-worm's liver.
Whin aa' thing went as he hed planned
   He steered back loop b' loop:
The aald folk say that he meed land
   Below the banks o' Noup.
     Some dazed lik' yet plaesed lik',
     I hinno muckle doot;
      T'ough dare'n, aye faer'n
     If he wad e'er win oot.

Whit happened efter maaks a teel:
Lang pairts o' it I mind on weel
   (A'm h'ard it aft in Redland).
Hid's forkie tongue raise ower the mune,
Brak aff, and then cam' tumblan doun
   'Twixt Norawa an' Swed-land.
Alang the sea i' twisted lumps
   Yin serpent form wis hurled,
An' twisted roond wi' siclik thumps
   As aa' but couped the world.
     Wi' crunchan an' munchan
   Hid's teeth fell oot in whiles,
     Cam' rumblan an' tumblan
   Tae mak wir Orkney isles.

At lang-last in a fair torment
The monster in contortions went,
   Sae sweean wis hid's liver.
Aald Stoor-worm knotted in a coil,
An fae hid's mooth the lowan oil
   Cam' straeman lik' a river.
Yin toonsfolk hinno muckle sense:
   They ca' it a volcano.
But faith, me neem is Willie Spence,
   Wae spaek o' whit we ken o'.
     Sic havers an' clavers!
   It aa' tuk pläce, wha kens.
     Aye, laugh thoo! A'm aff noo
   Tae maet me twa'rthree hens.

Shore Poems

and other Verse

Lost Self

To be what I have been but am no more
Or find the shadow of what once was plain
I pace the margin of this haunted shore
Where rocks and stones and echoing cliffs retain
Lost ecstasies, and shouts of natural joy.
Back through a maze of transient gains and griefs
I pick my steps to seek a phantom boy
Who flits from ledge to ledge on these black reefs.
But all the pools have unfamiliar grown
Since those forgotten years, nor can I trace
The distant footprints there that are my own,
Which time can never touch nor tides efface.
    Of this strange world the meaning who can tell,
    Receding thus from those that know it well?

Birsay Shore

The night of storm and fate,
In the receding hour
To voider darkness caught,
Is reft from love and hate.
I see the hollow Tower,
See it, and see it not.

The summer wind that blows
On hearths that are no more,
And in the silence saith
Words from another shore,
Brings not upon its breath
Time's dispetalled rose.

The stones that fall and fell
Are sunk in loathsome weeds
And fill the crystal well.
But why it should be so
None either asks or heeds:
It was so long ago.

The broken gable walls
Like fingers clutch the sky,
But never can lay hold
Of what is past and told.
The empty palace halls
Are here, and all gone by.

All ghosts that vanish so
North, south, west and east,
Yet will not from us go,
Battle and revel feast —
These in this air are seen
As though they had not been.

Shore Grave

Once again, where they found you
And your shore-tossed bones were laid,
The wet sea-sand above you
Is trenched by an iron spade.

Lightly you lie there, coffined
In rude slabs from the beach,
Where the storms of winter are breaking
And sea-gulls wail and screech.

Your skull is brown and fragile,
Sentient even in death,
As if it felt the salt wind
And once again drew breath.

Your hollow dark eye-sockets
Look out towards the sea,
And the shadows within them flicker
With thought's strange mystery.

Ear to the ground, you are waiting
For the sea's far summons still,
Fain to confront the ocean
With a seaman's eager skill.

Out on the height of the yard-arm
You are wrestling with the gale,
Your finger-bones still clutching
For rope and spar and sail.

Rest there in your narrow cabin
As once in some timbered hull
Your head was pillowed as calmly
As now your sleeping skull.

Freed from the cold agony
Of the slow devouring wave
And the pitiless rage of the tempest,
Quit not your sheltered grave.

Sleep on in this pleasant foreshore
Where fishers come and go,
While over your head the sea-pinks
And wild sea-grasses grow.

Morning Wave

Again, and yet again, in stately height
The smooth Atlantic breakers, one by one,
   Quicksilvered by the shining morning sun,
And by the wind's swift fingers polished bright,
Mirror the fabulous firmament of light.
   Look there, it is a strange phenomenon —
   For the green shutters fall, and what was won
In that brief glance, foam curtains from our sight.

What power, against Time's flux, did there engrave
The sun's escutcheon on the dying wave?
   Seal and re-seal? What feet that instant flew
Winged with mercurial strength, and leaping, spanned
The empyrean gulf? Or what chance hand
   Held up that burnished glass? those curtains drew?

Old Jeems

I knew a Birsay man, an old beachcomber
Who gathered driftwood, holding it in scorn
To lose one piece. His thoughts, like those of Homer,
Compassed the ocean. Oft by memory borne
On long sea voyages around the Horn,
He saw the storm waves sweep the high four-master,
Or caught some glimpse of shipwreck and disaster
Beyond the latitudes of Capricorn.

And so beside his woodpile he would stand
When evening came, and lost in distant dreams
Gaze seaward, motionless, with pipe in hand.
Beside him, too, now finished with their labours
Would come for idle talk his friendly neighbours:
For everyone about the P'lace knew Jeems.

Shore Companions

I am no alien here, nor do I walk
    These grassy banks in vacant solitude.
Along the geo the eider leads her brood
Where ragged foam fringes the shelving rock.
The friendly seal, swimming amid the shock
    Of breaking seas, plunges to seek its food;
    Or landward lifts its head in curious mood:
I whistle – and it listens to my talk.

Along the tidemark piping voices run
    And seabirds congregate. Into my sight,
Towards the burn-mouth, now that day is done,
    The heron comes with slow ungainly flight.
The very cows that graze the cliff-top grass
Lift up their heads and watch me as I pass.

In the Ebb

Even upon the margin of the deep
    Life spills her myriad forms before our gaze
    In tiny treasures – bright anemones,
Worms, star-fish, crabs, and little fish that leap
Across the pools. Look how storm waves heap
    A fringe of shell along these sandy bays,
    And how on golden bladderweed that sways
With rhythmic motion periwinkles creep.

I step from stone to stone, and as I peer
    Far into depths of pools inhabited
By swarming ocean creatures, I can hear
    Echoes around me of the Voice that said,
Go, have dominion over great and small,
And name all living things that swim or crawl.

Birsay in Winter

No, it is not the wealth of summer flowers,
    Eyebright and sea-pink, or the drifts of shell
    Heaped by the waves – though these delight me well —
That interfuse with joy the timeless hours.
Even in winter, when the driving showers
    Sting hands and face, and the long Atlantic swell
    Murmurs with menacing floods, I feel the spell
Of this wild coast, and its mysterious powers.

Cliff-top and stubble field, now bleached and bare,
    Hold fast their strength. Daylong the storm-tide pounds
      The bouldered beach; and I, so held in thrall
By sense of things not seen, but blindly stare
    (Within the shelter of the old sea-wall)
    Out on the sea's expanse and glimmering bounds.

Sea Monsters

Wild dervish winds upon the tempest ride.
    Shoreward, with dragon jaws, the storm waves leap
    And bite the rocks. Sea gods rich bounties heap
Up Viking geos – old treasures, tossed aside
Beneath great beanstalk cliffs. Strange monsters glide
    Sunwise in druid circle through the deep
    Or else, with dipping motion, bask asleep
In gentle summer calms upon the tide.

From what invisible land beyond the bounds
    Where sky and ocean (far as eye can reach)
      Mingle in luminous light, do thus uprise
Those fabulous beasts? and whence those ominous sounds
      Of birds in flight that mourn with woeful cries
    Heraldic dolphins stranded on the beach?

The Happy Fisherman

Within his little kingdom
Beside the Birsay shore
He's tilled his few green acres
For thirty years or more,
Yet even at his farm-work
He listens to the roar
Of great Atlantic breakers,
And wanders back and fore
With eye upon the weather
Until the gods restore
The longed-for hours of sea work,
Handling creel and oar.
He's ready every evening,
Cuithe wands at the door,
Returning nigh on midnight
With ten to twenty score,
And lythe, perhaps, from Marwick
To salt and lay in store.
Thus Willie, for a lifetime
Skilled in country lore,
Has ruled his little kingdom
Beside the Birsay shore.

Angle of Vision

But, John, have you seen the world, said he,
Trains and tramcars and sixty-seaters,
Cities in lands across the sea —
Giotto's tower and the dome of St. Peter's?

No, but I've seen the arc of the earth,
From the Birsay shore, like the edge of a planet,
And the lifeboat plunge through the Pentland Firth
To a cosmic tide with the men that man it.

Fossils and Fish

From all that death has clutched
The envious years have made
A cliff that may be touched,
And from forgotten shores
Layer on layer laid
Of fondly-misered stores.

The living flesh and bone
Here are held in stone.
Sinew and nerve and brain
Move not nor feel nor talk:
Birds beat their wings in vain,
And fishes swim in rock.

But on this other side,
A world of wild escapes —
Where float and gleam and glide
Creatures weirdly fleshed
In antique protean shapes
That will not be enmeshed.

Here, life has quite undone
All that death has won,
And still in purple deeps
The infinite pattern keeps
Of logarithmic form
In wave and shell and storm.

The Stone Wave

On this great beach a wild
                Atlantic storm
Sculptures in stone its huge
                and wavelike form.

New Cemetery, Birsay

Struck by Death's storm, this
                churchyard's even ground
Breaks its green calm with many
                a wavelike mound.

People and Places

Orkney Historian

Though all his days were given to meet the needs
Of country folks with farm manures and seeds,
He saw the islands chiefly as a place
Haunted by heroes of an ancient race,
Watched Viking longships sailing down the String
And earls contending at the island Thing.

A Bygone Kirkwall Gardener

He knew each plant and garden flower,
Cocked a shrewd eyebrow in his labours,
Wrote books, and in his dinner hour
Made merry quips with passing neighbours.

The Miller

By day he laboured in the mill
And in the evening fished for trout:
He was a man of patient skill
Who loved his task, indoors or out;
And nothing better to his taste
Than when his evening board was graced
With new bere bannocks and a fry
Of sweet half-pounders caught on fly.

On Sigurd —

WHO GAVE A FIELD AS A GRAVEYARD

Here, in his own home field, among his guests,
Crofters and fishermen, old Sigurd rests.

Burgess Ticket

15TH DECEMBER, 1954

In slow procession
Invisible and mute
The centuries crowd in —
No drum's incessant din,
Fanfare, or salute.

Look how they come! —
Thronging arch and aisle;
And we, as held in thrall
Through this strange interval,
Silent the while.

Helmed Jorsalafarers,
Magnus, martyr slain,
Earls of high renown,
Banner and shield and gown,
Rognvald and Sweyn.

The great rose window
Pours down its hallowed light,
Scattering tinctured stains:
See there, beyond its panes,
Wings raven black in flight.

Comes the high moment.
Beside the lofty pier
Stands the honoured guest,
Midmost among the rest —
The centuries are here.

Evening Landscape

Caught in a magical web, from the bus
I watch the familiar view: brown moor
Patched emerald, and fields grown fabulous
With yellow stooks; mountains in miniature
Held in translucent ecstasy; a land
Where hornèd cows – in pools metallic bright —
Cut out in black against green meadows stand,
And flocks of homing pigeons take their flight.
All suddenly takes meaning: for the sun
Descends – and sky, lochs, farms, and distant sea
(Amethyst and purple) merge in one,
Dwelling again in love and harmony,
    As if their Maker's first beatitude
    Came down the hills "How pleasant and how good!"

Orkney

To my Uncle William

This is the land whereon our fathers wrought
    Year after year, feeling scant need to clutch
    For distant gains, since, with little or much,
They tilled their scattered fields as they'd been taught,
Or tried the sea to find what might be caught
    Of fish or crab. This was their land, and such
    Their joy therein, seeing the sunlight touch
Its evening hills, no other land they sought.

This kingdom, too, is ours, and in our blood
    Its passionate tideways run: its moorlands fill
With peace our casual eyes; and the wild flood
      Of winter haunts our ears with spells that bind
    Sea, sky, and earth in one. Each cliff and hill
      Lies like a shadow on the brooding mind.

The Seeing Eye

Too long through hidden landscapes of the mind
    The seeing eye, snared by pale ghosts that pass,
    Holds in itself as in a crystal glass
Troops of thin shadowy forms, and I am blind
To all those visible delights that bind
    Man's sense with beauty – fields of waving grass,
    Bright skies, and happy foreshores. Those, alas,
Dissolve in dream and vanish undefined.

Loosed from such inward bonds I now regain
    An eye whose vagrant flights of late have been
        Hemmed in by pallid thought, by pen and book.
        Slowly at first, but with a swiftening look
It leaps across great miles of moorland plain,
    Up hillside steeps, and down through valleys green.

Renewal

Look how my autumn leaves from green to gold
   Burn in their frosty fire. Tissue and vein
   Shiver and curl to ash: no flowers remain
On withered stem, or from the patient mould
Draw breath and on life's tree their fans unfold.
   Twice has my summer pride waxed high; now wane
   The gentle influences of the rain,
The sun, the earth: and death comes, dank and cold.

But fast inscalloped in the undying root,
   Constant beyond all change of sky or soil,
Lies fenced the mystery of the living shoot —
   Green involutions of the mind. No toil
   Attends their weaving. Ah, would they uncoil
Again from that inmost core, leaf, stem, flower, fruit.

The Artist

He took a plough for a palette knife, an island
For his canvas, primed by wind and weather.
Faded designs of moorland browns and yellows
Were scored upon its surface, cancelled markings
Of ancient artistry by ruder craftsmen.
Upon great fields of abstract composition
He laid a thick impasto, ridged and furrowed,
Then used his crops for colour – rows of turnip
Bright emerald green, and golden corn for sunshine,
Soft meadow hay for delicate bronze and russet,
Touched here and there with scarlet; and for figures
Placed in his picture's foreground sheep and cattle,
　　Year after year his landscape rearranging,
　　Baffled to catch perfection's changing shadow.

In Dumfries Museum

Five hundred million years ago (they said)
Reptilian toes, in times outspanning time,
For us impressed upon the cosmic slime
These hieroglyphic foot-prints; see how claws
Of creatures now invisible and dead
Record the swift pursuit, and trace on stone
The ancient terrors loosed by Nature's laws.
And on this other slab swift ripples moan
From winds that raged beside an ancient shore
Where no man ever sailed or dipped an oar.
Far out of time we yet can hear them blow,
These winds – five hundred million years ago.

Microcosm of Beauty

I came to see the lofty mountain peaks:
It was the little things that held my gaze.
The alpine rose, the wild anemones,
And small green mountain lizards. Beetles, too,
And butterflies competed with the view,
l could have watched these little things for weeks,
And smiled to see, contending for the eye,
A mountain challenged by a butterfly.

Two Seas

Lies now upon this home of sleeping gales
A radiant pool of light, as if below
Great shoals were moving to and fro
Agleam with silver scales.

Yet as I watch, again in thought I go
By Adriatic deeps whose surface hides
Fish rainbow-tinted, and whose tides
In muted colour flow.

Train Journey

Journeying homeward, from my corner seat
    I watch the view beside the railway lines.
    It passes like a film: olives and vines
Lacing the landscape; strips of sugar beet
Hoed by Italian peasants; fields of wheat
    Scarlet with poppies; strange commercial signs
    And white-washed farms. Far off, the Apennines
Shimmer, blue-distanced in the summer heat.

Beyond it all I see an island shore
    Far in the north – the land that I love best.
    Again I gather sea-shells on the Brough,
Or dream an angler's dream and drift once more
    Within my little boat, when on the loch
    Trout rise, and the wind blows from the west.

Other Shores

The Title

*"Let Christ the King of Israel descend now
from the cross, that we may see and believe."
Mark 15.32.*

Forth from Zion's citadel
Who is this led out to die,
As those voices rise and swell
"Crucify Him – crucify!"?
Mocking rulers make reply,
"Christ the King of Israel!"

Simon, whom they did compel
After Him to bear His cross,
Saw His anguish and could tell
How the soldiers dice did toss,
How He died to bear our loss —
Christ the King of Israel.

Hushed be every heart and tongue!
There, to save our souls from hell,
He in agony is hung,
Numbered thus with thieves among.
'Twas for us – O mark it well —
Christ, the King of Israel.

Like a wounded wild gazelle,
Stricken sore and mortally,
From His parchèd lips there fell
Groans of dire extremity:
"Why hast Thou forsaken Me —
Christ the King of Israel?"

Finished what the Scripture saith
And the prophets' words foretell:
Silenced now each infidel.
See! He bows His head in death,
And He yields His parting breath —
Christ, the King of Israel.

Here, beside His cross, is found
Mercy without parallel.
This indeed is holy ground,
Let our sandals be unbound
While we linger near its spell —
Christ the King of Israel.

Praises be for what befell
On that dark and dreadful day.
Everywhere let people say
"This our guilty fears can quell:
Christ has borne our sins away —
Christ the King of Israel."

Hail we Him, Emmanuel,
Throned upon the royal tree,
Who in distant islands dwell;
And from henceforth none but He
Shall our God and Saviour be —
Christ, the King of Israel.

Thine Evermore

"Thine are we, David, and on thy side, thou son of Jesse"
I Chronicles 12.18.

Lord, we are Thine, the captives of Thy bow:
Fast as we fled Thine arrows laid us low.
We found Thee Friend who feared Thee once as Foe.

Lord, we are Thine, necks bowed beneath Thy yoke,
Since first Thy goad our swift rebellion broke,
And Thou Thy gentle word of conquest spoke.

Lord, we are Thine, and shoulder Thy commands
Burdens laid there by Thee, who loosed our bands
And bore *our* heavy burden in Thy hands.

Captain of our salvation, staunch and tried,
Thine are we evermore, O Crucified!
Thine are we evermore, and on Thy side.

Lord of All

If into time time's Lord and Maker came
And on time's calendar pricked off the days;
If He to whom was said, Thou art the same,
In growth and wisdom suffered time's delays:
If He Himself, the mighty God, came down
Whose Presence fills the continents of space,
Assumed our mortal flesh, left heaven's renown,
And here on earth journeyed from place to place —
Then time and space that wholly frustrate seemed
Are subject to their King, and from the dead
By Him are borne in triumph and redeemed.
Now everywhere to men this word is said,
   Time bears the programme of eternity:
   Christ is the Sum of all things that shall be.

His Proper Work

He gives the mountains birth:
Light comes at His command,
Whose word upholds the shining Pleiades
And formed both sea and land:
He gladdens heaven and earth.
These, these are but the outskirts of His ways,
Whom angels serve and praise.
Across the firmament of many nations
His lightnings flash
And thunders crash,
Bursting with loud and long reverberations.
Clouds are His covering:
Above the world He sits as King,
And counts the isles a very little thing.

To all He giveth breath.
His hand lifts up the poor.
He seals love's writ to set the prisoner free
And pay sin's forfeiture:
He conquers hell and death.
This, this His proper work, which none but He
Can pledge or guarantee.
Down from the heights the Lord of all descended
Our grief to share.
We see Him there
Upon the cross by iron nails suspended.
From wounds incarnadine
Deep-marked with mercy's fivefold sign
The splendours of the triune Godhead shine.

Without God

From the German of Jochen Klopper

Without God I am a raindrop in the fire,
Without God a fish upon the strand,
Without God a sparrow whose wings tire,
And a blade of grass within the sand.
But when God calls me by my name,
I am air, water, earth, and flame.

Last Voyage

"Having a desire to depart" Philippians 1.23.

"The time of my departure is at hand." II Timothy 4.6.

Cast off, cast off the ropes!
Set course: and spite of fears
Hold for the open sea, to gain at last
The region of thy hopes.
Hoist up the trembling sails
With eager hands upon the ship's high mast.
Time for delay is past!
The dark-faced pilot waits.
With courage in thy heart
Make ready to depart.
Another Form is at the harbour gates
To welcome and escort
Each little vessel safely home to port.

The Hidden Land

Autumn Sunset

If it be so, that what I see and hear
On this autumnal coast is nothing more
Than sounding seas and rugged reef-bound shore,
Caught in the colour of the changing year —
Whence, then, transcending eye and listening ear,
Do thoughts arise within me that restore
Forgotten moods, and rouse me to explore
The hidden source of things that do appear?

Uptilted now, the sun's vast crucible
Pours out upon the waves its molten gold,
And evening light with gentle radiance falls
In benediction on the cliff's high walls;
Illuminate like these, I feel the spell
Of thrones invisible in all that I behold.

Marwick Head

You silent rocks, what have you given me?
Something has passed between us (this I know)
That makes me feel your strange identity
And all familiar sense of things forgo.
Was it when playing heedless on the shore,
In boyhood, that I caught your gifts? They came
Neither from sound nor sight, but were things more
Of spiritual essence, known without a name.
The years are not mistaken: some deep bond
Fast-forged in winter storm and summer air
So binds me to your strength, I pierce beyond
Mere forms, and ask your sea-cliffs ledged and bare
   "What unseen tides among those reefs of stone
    Claim kinship thus with nerve and brain and bone?"

The Encounter

Returning from the loch, nigh on midnight
Slowly the angler plods his way upstream
Among the reeds and rushes, as in dream,
Held in the hush of an Orkney twilight,
When all at once on the bank across the water
(Whether by deep design or blind chance)
Appeared at the stream's edge a full-grown otter,
Crouched in heraldic stance.

Stock-still one moment, then, suddenly released —
A splash, and it was gone, the spell broken;
But for a brief season it was a token
Of the ancient covenant 'twixt man and beast.

Homeward, once more, the fisher resumed his way,
Aware of this strange encounter; pre-ordained
To renew and restore what kinship, who could say? —
Else not to be explained.

The Sea-Mark

I

In the Museum of the Louvre
Stands an Egyptian tomb
Whose sepulchral room
Electric lamps illume.

Leading their cattle home
Pharoah's fellaheen
Yet can there be seen,
Angular and lean —

Herdsmen and their oxen,
Moving rank by rank:
Hands long and lank
Laid on head or flank.

II

Stanced with ritual space between them
A lone peasant and his team
Crowns the ridge – as had I seen them
In a time-dissolving dream.

Yoked in line along the furrow
The white oxen draw the plough.
To what mythic far tomorrow
Move they still as moving now?

Animals in linked succession
As upon a sculptured frieze
Pace the earth in slow procession
Near the sacred olive trees.

Wild hieratic motions making
Goes a maiden, arms outspread,
The long whip-lash backward snaking
In dark lightnings overhead.

Earth's springtime train, transmuted,
Changes with the changing, sun,
Yet the Delphic tree, deep-rooted,
Many-branched, remains but one.

III

Inshore fishers who embark
Oceanward, can oft divine
Some ancestral fishing mark
When two headlands come in line.

Spite of this I know not whether
Aught were there or was it chance
When two moments came together
From Italian fields and France.

The Masque

The black heraldic headland lifts its shield,
    But whose device it bears no man can tell,
Though blazoned clearly on an azure field —
    And simple fishers know its ledges well.

With hollow voice the ocean speaks its part,
    Now high, now low, and once again I ask
Whose tongue it is strikes terror in my heart,
    Or lulls my grief behind that painted mask.

Why hides itself in camouflage of green
    The ancient earth, whose continents we know?
What lies invisible, and is not seen,
    In rocks and iron, water, ice, and snow?

Tiptoe in cosmic dance the mantled moon
    And her attendant stars traverse the night.
To celebrate what deed, or for what boon
    They hold these revels, none can say aright.

Vainly in tragic posture weeps the rain:
    Too like a pageant are those gestures bold.
In vain the waves advance, the winds in vain
    Flourish their trumpets, clouds their flags unfold.

But I have seen, like treasure long concealed,
    A sudden radiance break from evening skies,
And everything on sea and shore and field
    In flawless essence move, without disguise;

And watched with awe, beside the old sea wall,
    In the hushed silence of a summer night,
O'er land and sea an innocent beauty fall —
    The setting sun had touched the world with light.

The Floss, Westray

Within its narrow bound,
This cottage by the shore,
With dark low lintelled door,
And all the little yards
Won from the sandy shards,
Is my ancestral ground.

Its walls are crystal clear
Though built of stone and clay,
And through them still appear
(Yet how, O who can say?)
The weaver at his loom
In a bare-walled room.

Sounds of grief and mirth
Echo from what has gone.
Beside the smouldering hearth,
Sits with ravelled hair,
In her straw-back chair,
A woman all alone.

Snug in shuttered beds
Children huddle in dream:
Of things long gone they seem
The stationary proof.
Upon their sleeping heads
Rain drips from the roof.

Forefathers, distant and near,
Beyond what I can trace
Crowd around me here,
Many a forgotten face
Which yet I never knew,
Although the vision be true.

Winter Sadness

Down earth's furrowed face
Weeps its way to the sea
This winter burn at the P'lace,
And dumbly shares with me
An inarticulate grief
That life should be so brief.

By beds of water-mint
And blue forget-me-not
Joy flowed in summer's prime,
And on bright shallows caught
A momentary glint
Of worlds untouched by time.

Dwells in this silent stream
A secret few can guess,
Deeper than thought can reach,
And by it I possess
An image of nature's dream —
There is no need for speech.

A Morning at Wasdale

Beside a quiet moor-clad hill
The burn flows down a rocky gill,
And where the waterfall descends
A friendly tree above it bends.

One April morning, as I stood
Watching there in solitude
Young daffodils on the bank below,
I saw a yellow-yorlin go.

Up from the pool beside the brig
It flew, and hung upon a twig,
As if in very joy of Spring
A daffodil had taken wing,

Or bud had blossomed on the tree
In rage of sudden rivalry.
It surely was a vision sent
To be a sign and sacrament.

> *Gone is that day, but still I see*
> *The bird fly up in ecstasy*
> *And perch upon the magic tree.*

Bees on Dandelions

A few late autumn dandelions
(Golden suns in a green sky)
Lift their heads in proud defiance
Though summer's noon is all gone by.

Bees, in thin sunshine, toil and slave,
Lest hidden nectar spoils be lost
And winter lock the Aladdin cave
With secret spell and key of frost.

Eastern Window

Experiments in Haiku

Evening

On a fencing post
    a grey owl sits:
        a summer day's ghost.

Sunset

In the West, a rose
    opens – and on the waves
        petal on petal throws.

Futility

November waves reach
    skyward: a drift of spent foam
        lies upon the beach.

Sea-Fog

White mists come and go
    upon the cliff-top: blind sounds
        rise up from below.

Sea Surface

Ah! – mirror shattered:
    sky's image lost, cloud fragments
        on wave-tops scattered.

Shipwreck

Masts gone, timbers splintered,
    a dark reef foam-flecked:
        sorrow here has wintered.

Eight O'Clock Bells

Magnus' bells beguile
    day into silence: listen!
        echoes from each isle.

In Viking Cathedral

Darkly on stained glass
    rooks throw shadows: long-boats
        with raven banners pass.

Last Obsequies

Hands on gunwale – to the noust
    haul this weathered yawl:
        there leave her, safely housed.

Newly Collected
Poems

The Sceptic

(After Horace)

Ill-thrawn wis I, an' scant o' grace;
God's ways I couldna thole nor trace,
    But gaed like wandered stirk
    Tae vildro through the mirk.

Blawn wi' aa airts, I drave afore,
An' weel-nigh wrecked on many a shore,
    'Mang sceptic notions veered —
    Sae wild a coorse I steered.

But in the hinmost depth o' need,
When life, it hung but b' a threed,
    I f'und the wey o' truth
    In lear o' early youth.

Noo ken I that there's Ane abune
Can wheep awey the monarch's croun,
    An' wi' a gentler hand
    Can Mercy's task command.

The Morning's Wark

"Three lapsters and a starfish,
  Wi' an odd partan or twa,
And a lang speel at the oars —
  That wis aa.

"Wae strave i' the lift o' the sea
  Oot tae the West'ard, and fegs,
The creels were aa driven in
  Tae the face o' the craigs.

"Seven and six apiece
  The lapsters'll fetch, maybe —
It's aye weel wrought for
  'At comes fae the sea."

The Impartial Sun

On meadow-girse and field o' bere
The reip'nan sun shines doun alike
And nourishes wi' equal care
Wild flowers apae this aald hill dyke.

The Plastics

The Plastics eyed wi' derision
   The slim wee book I printed
But the book till a third edition
   Suddenly sprinted.

It's sellan – craw nae croose!
   Withoot these gyte gymnastics;
Kailyairdie-like and doose,
   Nae like the Plastics.

[Fu' o' Bristles]

"Put it down a wee, my lord."
Let English dons with grand idears
Disdain the wisdom of the years
   And legislate for spellers:
Let Law revise the A.B.C.
And Sassenach bureaux, scorning "V",
   Reform their own Sam Wellers.
The Scots are made of sterner stuff,
   Brought up on brose and thistles.
They like their language really tough —
   Guid Lallans fu' o' bristles.
     The Plastics' gymnastics
       Fair fleg these Suthran critters,
    Aye mummlan and whumblan
      Wi' Jamieson lug-splitters.

Jeems's Welcome

Weel boy, thoo're heem!
An' are thoo fund aa
Whit thoo gaed tae seek?
Thoo're rubbid claes
Wae a' yin uncan folk
Wha spaek maist wae their haans,
Yet feenty wird a body kens when deun;
An' thoo'll be aeten
O' their furrin maet,
An' clean forgot the taste
O' partans an' bere bread.
Boy, boy.
An' a' yin kirks an' t'ings
Thoo gaed tae see,
Maybe the Pope himsel'
For a' I ken,
T'inks thoo he prays as weel
As wae deu i' the peerie Kirk
Abeun de Hill?
I kinno.
For a' the mountain grandeur
That thoo've seen
I wadna cose ae leuk
At the tide race at the Brough,
Or the soond o' the cullyas
Screaman' i' the teeth o' the wast win'.
Whit says thoo? – A' thee money's deun.
Whit odds, boy – thoo're been lang awa',
An' noo thoo're heem.
A'm blide.

1920

Mind thee thoom,
Or hid'll get nippid!
Aye, yin's the heddle
O thee grandfaither's loom.
Monie a pair
O' heem-meid blankets
He wrought apae it —
Eens that wad wear!
Whit wae his hens
An' bit keil-yaird
He meed a liveen
No muckle, thoo kens —
In yin days
They lived on tatties
An' pit on naught
Bit aald claes
Hid a horse, A'm h'ard,
An' did some cairteen —
Boats – ballast —
Fae the sandy shard.
He's lang deid
An' buried, for the aald wife
Wi' the lang shears
Clippid his threed.
Aye, A'm hin it noo
Thae haep o' years;
An' heth, hid's workan —
A'maist geud as new!
Hid gaed for the price o' a nowt
At the sell-up o' the Floss —
The loom thee grandfaither wrouwt.

Willie's Boat

Aye, yin's her wi' the green paint,
Twal'-feet keel – and a grand seaboat.
Spier no' the 'oors afloat
'At I in her hae spent.

Mony a time, when tides were low
A'm haaled her doun ower the sand,
Pit nile-pin in, and wi' a hand
Apae the gunwale, teen the geo.

A'm noo – near as I can tell —
Haen her for forty year or more
Handled her wi' thole-pin an' oar
Till she's pairt o' mesel'.

Her timmers like me ain – decayed,
An' the warse o' wer – are almost deun.
Baith hae haen their day, and seun
Must in the noust be laid.

Gather Ye Groaties

I sowt hid a hale tideswater
Bit never a een fand I,
An' a' I got for me pains
Wis scrubbid knees an' a breeksed back.
Me Grandfaither said
"Boy, if thoo finds a groatie
Thee fortune's meed, an' thoo'll
Never need tae wirk a ferm
Or geung on the sea."
An' than the tide cam' ap
An' covered a' the shore.
There he fand me sittan
Wae me tinnie aside me
Abeun the banks.
"Whit fan' thoo boy?" spiered he
For I wis close tae gowlan,
An' coppid oot the tinnie
On the girse;
"A peerie crab, twa-t'ree whelks,
An' five cattie buckies —
No a fortune Robbie,
Bit something teu.
Cheust luk thoo at the crab
Hoo weel his joints wirk,
An' hoo he's coloured that
He'll no be seen,
An' look thoo at thee buckies,
Wha mowlded them?
Thir's no a man in Orkney
That could mak' een gin he tried.
They're Nature's jewels min,

Flung oot tae us wae a lavish han'.
An' hid's ta'en the patience
O' ten million years
Tae mak' the sand oot there
Whar the waves dunder,
An' yet min', hid's a' numbered,
Every single grain.
Dis that no' teach thee something?
Patience min, patience,
Thoo're far ower hurried.
The tide geungs oot again
An' thoo can hunt the morn."
Me Grand-faither
He wis a wise man.
Bit a' the sam'
I never fand een.
Gather ye groaties while ye may
Before the tide comes in,
For Robert never thinks to stop
Till the water laps his chin!
No use to him are rubber boots,
Nor the waders that he carries,
For if he once begins to hunt
He tarries, tarries, tarries.

"Mac Pherson o' the Glen"

"Mac Pherson o' the Glen," in oils – tae ilka person
Wha sweengs a kilt hoo like it is, except Mac Pherson.

A Bachelor Looks at the Wedding Presents

Inside a hoose the ither day
A haep o' wedding presents lay.
They covered floor and chairs and bedstead
And I, with shakings of the head said,
    "I never saa the like o' this.
    O what a thing is married bliss!"

Warm sheets and blankets filled the room,
    Down quilts and pillow-cases.
It's little wonder bride and groom
    Hae got such happy faces.

There's pots and pans, and forks and knives,
    Grand plates and Pyrex dishes
Enough tae dae a score o' wives
    And show their friends' good wishes.

Jist look aroond on a' this store
    Canteens wi' spoon and ladle —
Room clocks – and many a fine thing more
    But tell me – where's the cradle?

Weel, for a man tae hae a wife
    Maun hae its compensations
If nothing else, when things are rife
    It learns him tae hae patience.

It is a noble state, nae doot
Times shachlan in an auld dish cloot.
I think I'll stick tae fishing troot
    Just look at yon poor cratur
Pushing aa' day in Sunday suit
    A great big pramulator.

We bachelors wha roam sae free
Fae place tae place, fae sea tae sea
Can only wonder when we see
    The young folk sae demented
"What's that!" I hear you say to me,
    "Man, if he only kent it!"

And so we wish the happy pair
Long life, good health and muckle mair
May each of them show mutual care
    And live in peace together
And years mak' none the worse o' wear
    Their love for ain anither.

An Orkney Romance

O' a' the parish lads o' Stennis
There's ane puir callant, wha, I ken, is
This meenit sufferin' frae a menace
   O' lass sae bonnie
Clean gluffed that his wee but and ben is
   Threatened wi' ony.

His surname – we maun be discreeter,
And simply say, it rhymes wi' Peter,
Her feet than his were somewhat neater
   She was a peach
And tae her laddie (never leet her)
   Stuck like a leech.

Was ever such a tangled ploy
The lass hersel' fair plagues the boy
Wha' fae his hame at Petersquoy
   Each fortnight's ending —
The scuddling loon – gings tae the toon
   For feckless spending.

Sly crounies most politely coughed.
Poor Jeems felt nabbid as they doffed
Their mocking caps, but back she scoffed
   "We're weel acquaint."
Less lees – the victim muttered soft,
   "I might hae kent it."

At last the sore tormented creatur
Said, "Fegs, me boys, ah'm gan tae cheat 'er
Ah'll shove some pooshun o salt-petre
    In her cup coffee
Jeems, lad, if tha'll nae defeat her
      'Am no worth toffee."

In Icey's shop he next did meet her.
Quoth Jeems, "I doot ah'll hae tae treat 'er.
Ah'm fairly copped, but, heth, ah'll beat her
    Or Ah'm nae Jeemie."
Soon fae the girl cam oot a skirl,
      "Ah'm feelan' squeamy."

"Ha! ha!" laughed he, "Ye brazen slut
Nae mair through Kirkwall lanes we'll strut."
"O Jeemie, lad," she wailed, "we're cut
    For matrimony."
"Na! Na!" says he, "it's naething but
    A matter o' money."

Up then she jumped with "Hey diddle diddle
Heighho me lads! Let him sky diddle,
I've twa three mair strings tae me fiddle
    I'll soon be tredding
In bridesmaid's shoes to solve love's riddle
    At Ruby's wedding."

Magnus, the Martyr

On Egil's isle the Viking chiefs held tryst:
    'Twas Eastertide, when God's mild mercy made
    Revenge of private wrong be wholly stayed,
Up-pointing to the patient suff'ring Christ.
Beyond an earldom's title Magnus priced
    Orcadia's tranquil rule; and unafraid,
    Hailed faithless Hacon, knelt him down and prayed —
Renouncing all, with God's good Will sufficed.

The high-swung axe a mighty death-wound hewed;
    The kingly martyr bowed before his fate:
    The red blood flowed, fast quenching Hacon's hate
Long kindled from the flame of ancient feud.
    Ye Christians, learn! Your warlike pride abate:
When evil threatens, overcome with good.

On First Seeing 'Linklater and Greig'

Emergent from the sea in ruthless height,
    Propped on its elbow leans the huge cliff wall,
    Like some primeval giant held in thrall
Raising his form in slow malignant might.
Around those waves great sea-floods, swirling white,
    With vast impetuous motions rise and fall,
    And gathering strength, up-leap with sudden squall
Against the snowy sea-birds poised in flight.

Swung on the ocean swell, 'twixt cliff and rock,
Behold how in their stout-ribbed fishing boat
Two seamen of the ancient Viking stock
    Ride o'er the crested waves, defying fate.
In Orkney's native element they float,
    Eye, hand, and human will co-ordinate.

Motor Run to Birsay October 1949

Everyone was in the fields that day
Forking up or building stacks:
We saw them as the car sped its way,
Country women, old men with bowed backs,
Lifting their tatties, and into sacks
Filling heaped pailfuls; while on each field
Snorting engines, ploughing furrowed tracks,
Down the drill scattered the season's yield.
Suddenly a wisdom was revealed,
Old as Eden, bound fast to the soil.
Men, strong-handed, Nature's forces wield,
Banishing all bondage from such toil.
    We, like gods remote on Heaven's high hill,
    Saw it afar as a brave spectacle.

Birsay in Winter

No, no, I much prefer the wild sea-pinks
To Birsay's winter shore, for I rebel
Against those odours – don't I know them well! —
Of rotten seaweed with its horrid stinks.
Before the stench imagination shrinks
For not a disinfectant can dispel
Its rank effluvium. Fauch! the awful smell
Comes floating now across the grassy links.

Foul thick miasmas round the houses hang,
And at the burnmouth, even I, alas,
Must hold my nose for smell of putrid tang.
The very cows that graze the cliff-top grass
Lift up their heads and give a doubtful sniff.
Phew! Once again I feel that dreadful whiff!

Tradition

The islands voyage on, and in our sight
A wake behind them stretches, foaming white.

Plane Crash in Hoy

Into this land of silence and wonder
Where bog-asphodel gleams in the heather
And summer mists hang light as a feather
On bare hill tops, there roared with thunder
The friendly dragon. Ah! what mad blunder
Struck it then? Freak of whimsy or weather?
What doom? – for pilot and plane together
Crashed on the moorland: fell, torn asunder.

All things altered as if enchanted:
Pools aluminium bright, becoming
Metallic wreckage; like a muffled humming
Of insects, propellor blades were whirring;
Wild gullies turned into runways that slanted
With perilous dip, fresh panic stirring.

In Birsay

In tiny flowers on the links
Saw Soutar here when but a boy,
Immortal blossomings of joy?
And in these clumps of wild sea-pinks
A thing that death could not destroy?

Our Edwin, too, with quiet eyes,
Looked seaward from this narrow place
And in the gleam of Birsay skies
With poet's inward sight could trace
The ancient bounds of Paradise.

Here, too, when they their exile mourned,
They oft in silent thought returned.
"Happy," they said, "who never leave
That land, and have not cause to grieve
A loss which nothing can retrieve."

A Day in Kirkwall, 1759

Rising betimes, they made an early start,
    Got through their morning work, and had their meat —
    Then set out for the town. Some went on feet,
Leisurely travelling in from every part
And parish, east and west; some yoked the cart,
    And lumbered on (front-board for handy seat)
    Until at last they reached the narrow street
And drove their sheep and cattle to the mart.

They talked of this and that, were ready to discuss
The smacks discharging at the harbour head,
    Weather and price of crops, and foreign wars,
    Or how the wedding went, and who was dead —
    These nameless ghosts, our fabled ancestors,
Were they at all so different, then, from us?

Birsay Sunset

Day's exit behold!
    two silent headlands guarding
        a gateway of gold.

Orkney Sunset

All day long, tight-lipped, the visible world
Spoke not a word of saint or seraphim
And not a single shining token gave
Of fabulous lands beyond the ocean's rim.

But in the evening, when the sun went down,
And cloudy curtains trembled upon the skies
The far horizon opened like the rose
That blossoms in the meads of Paradise.

The View

My cottage window
Looks down to the foot of the garden,
Where a few flowers grow
Just beyond the tide's reach.
Then comes the burnmouth,
Foaming among its boulders;
And away to the south,
Headland and far horizon
Frame the sloping beach.
Everything is here: running waters,
Sea and sky, land and shore —
The whole world in miniature.

Prehistoric Monster

Emergent from the deep
Hoy rears her saurian form.
Stromness lies asleep.

Derelict Cottage: Pierowall

Fallen beams, bare rooms
And broken walls – but look!
Riot of garden blooms.

Portrait

Sketched with minimum
Of time, head and figure:
Two hours to do the thumb!

Stromness

Huddle of roof-tops, steep lanes;
A jigsaw of cubes,
Triangles and planes.

Sunset [2]

Mourn not the sun's demise
See how the clouds
Gather radiance from the skies.

The Wreck

See, she lies awash on this inshore skerry.
Masts and rigging still are in proud defiance
Held aslant like spears, as the foaming breakers
      Crash on her bulwarks.

Grieve nor mourn this loss, for around the headland
Builders' yards are busy, and ship-wrights fashion
Timbered keel and planking – again to venture
      Hostage to fortune.

Soon, come storm or calm, will the happy vessel
Seek the open sea, and with wild abandon,
Scorning reef and tideway and hidden skerry
      Swing down through Hoy Sound.

Stromness [2]

A Picture in Verse

Stromness! – a town whose cobbled highway remains
An artist's delight, with its huddle of houses and lanes
Composing a picture of cubes, triangles and planes.

Daily, with leisurely pace, through its long narrow street
Housewives from hillside and sea-front their shopping
    complete,
And neighbours abroad in friendly intercourse meet.

Morning by morning, fishermen gather their gear,
Make for the sea – and homeward, at eventide, steer
Each to his mooring or private stone-causey'd pier.

Hoy, with its sinuous ridges, weathered and scarred,
Up from the ocean emerges like saurian guard,
And over the slumbering town keeps innocent ward.

The Bay, Birsay

With gaping jaws this sharp-toothed Orkney strand
Snatches in greedy haste the ocean's hand.

Birsay Sunset [2]

Petalled upon the waves and clouded west
    The far horizon opens like a rose.
But by what ecstasy of light possessed,
    Or in what field it blossoms no one knows.

Is it a pageant or a silver screen —
    Whose glittering spears illume the evening sky?
Or is it some immortal fable seen
    Of things more real than meet the outward eye?

For pictured there in colours crystalline
    Are radiant forms that insubstantial seem,
And in their changing shapes become a sign
    Of mysteries caught sight of but in dream.

      In hall of mirrors cunningly confined,
      What do I see? Vision of eye or mind?

Orkney Sunset [2]

The sky was curtained at day's close,
When suddenly I saw with sun-enchanted eyes
The far horizon open like a rose
That blossomed in the meads of Paradise.

Upon the dancing wave and evening cloud
Were then a thousand crimson petals strewn,
And beauty into Time's sad furrows ploughed,
From mortal blight and dull decay immune.

Orkney's Beauty

Since poets praise those far climes in whose glades
    Swift tropic wings keep flight with old romance,
Praise Indian forests and Arabian shades
    In haunting music; since, with roving glance,
The home-returnèd sailor tells his tale
    Of golden countries, far across the sea,
Holding the beauty found in stream and vale
    Enough why these far lands should honoured be;
And since, O treeless Orkney, thou art set
    Where neither fragrant groves nor gardens are,
I'll weave for thee a prouder coronet —
    More worthy thou of praise than lands afar! —
These from themselves their valleys beautify,
But thine the loveliness of sea and sky.

Evening Watch, Scapa Flow

(On H.M.S. "Imperieuse")

Never can I forget that winter night
There on the upper deck so long ago,
When, idly gazing on the sea below,
I saw the ripples dance with silver light.
Dumbly I stood, transfixed before that sight —
It was a miracle, sent to foreshow
How sea and sky would yet together flow
In swift perpetual change of dark and bright.

But what the vision meant was never clear,
Nor could I read the metaphor in its place.
Aloft, the moon pursued her shining track
With brooding mien and ceremonial pace,
And on the sea's vast surface, velvet black,
Scattered her argent brilliance far and near.

Orkney After the War

Now from the pool the tide of war recedes
And upon the water's surface filtered falls
The old tranquillity. Wave the green sea-weeds
Fanning their fronds fearless of sudden squalls.
Old patient limpets scythe the meads aquatic
And rosy crinoids radiate starry twinkles
While hermit crabs with scuttlings acrobatic
Dispute the tenancy of vacant periwinkles.
    Merchant anemones spread their hungry tentacles
    And earnest cattie-buckies keep their social conventicles.

On Air

Window of light! Oh precious atmosphere.
   Thy wind-swept freshness fiercely we inhale
   With nostrils wide, extended to the gale.
Exultant then, we tread, with eye more clear,
Along the whiteness of the dusty road,
   And on the far horizon we descry
   The solitary steeple 'gainst the sky
Near sunlight mists which cover our abode.

Evening's Casement

In hushed serenity, the dusk of eve
   Imposes silence on this northern bay.
   Beside the water's edge so long I stay
That senses of faint motions round me heave.

Allured by those suggestions they receive,
   Sight's dim perceptions in an airy way
   To provinces of luminous ether stray
Till all the solid worth of earth they leave.

On such a night as this the soul might gain
   Unwanted freedom. Ranging to and fro,
The fervour-kindled eyes, in frenzied pain

   Hold distant tracts, which, through yon afterglow,
In fine day-tempered beauty, o'er the main,
   From evening clouds, long purple shadows throw.

Costa Head

I stand entranced beneath th'embattled height
    Of ocean cliffs, round whose broad shoulders cling
    Loose trailing vapours. Waves are whispering
A weeping mermaid's lone romantic plight.
Like tow'ring prophets wrapped in robes of light,
    Those crags on me a wild enchantment fling.
The living rock, the sea, and everything
Take airy voices. O to hear aright!

Before the glory bathing hill and steep
    An inward sense to finer feeling yields.
    Old Neptune, from a foamy billow, wields
His mighty trident o'er the sounding deep.
    While earth remains, and beauty fills the fields,
Be mine a soul whose vital pulses leap.

Early Snow

Like comely beggar maid
Around her shivering form
Earth drew her scanty plaid —
Threadworn it was and frayed —
Against November storm.

Riding in cavalcade
Winter to pity woke
And stooping undismayed
His royal ermine cloak
Across her shoulder laid.

A Blackbird's Soliloquy

An unfledged blackie here I lie
Under a bank of yellow clay.
Yet round the world, this morn in May
None happier than I.
In a wattled nest of common hay
Beside the burn and underneath
A greening clump of overhanging heath
I leapt to the light of day.

Rainbowed in a dewdrop's prism
The morning floods of daylight sink
Through tufted grass and heather chink,
A sunny cataclysm.
Lightly o'er the utmost brink
Of a broadening plantain blade
A crawling insect ventures unafraid.
I watch, with never a wink.

Hark. A cheerful carolling.
The thrush his mate is calling.
Once more comes down the morning music falling
From a laverock on the wing.

The Shepherd

Winter, dogs at heel,
Firmly in hand,
Slips the leash, whistles,
Gives word of command.
Belly-down on the sea
The storm winds are up,
And the islands huddle together
Like frightened sheep.

Abbey Craigs

I walked along a woodland path that wended
    By ancient boulders lichen-decked and grey
    Whose weathered forms like giant ramparts lay
Near to the crag's bald edge, o'er which impended
A beech-tree's venturous boughs. The sunshine blended
    Tall stems of oak with cornfields far away,
    But turned I to the inner woods to stray
Where shadowy trees to deeper glooms descended.

Before me opened vistas more entrancing
    Than magic glades by Attic bards avowed;
    While overhead there hung a golden cloud.
Then in my rest upon a volume chancing
    Of England's laurelled muse, I read aloud
A lovely song that set my spirit dancing.

Written after Reading
Matthew Arnold's Poems

A tinkling cascade, leaping from the height
    Sweet silver music making: this was h e
    Whose plaintive cadence, delicate and light
    Is but the voice of waters flowing free
From secret mountain springs. With aery vault
    The flashing fountain falls, and by our feet
Trickles a bubbling brook near which we halt,
    Tired and thirsty from our journey's heat.
'Tis ever thus! The poet's simple song
    Fringing the highway of life's pilgrimage
Heals and refreshes, makes us once more strong,
    And laughingly our madness doth assuage.
But upward look, and scan the untrodden brink
Whence issues this fair stream: stoop, then, and drink.

To the Nightingale

O Nightingale whom England's poets praise,
    What though – alas – I've never heard thee singing,
    In them, thy bards, like echoes wildly ringing
I seem to catch thy keen impassioned lays.
I ope my book, and lo! – 'mid leafy sprays,
    Thy warbled song its melody diffuses,
    Broadcasted to the world by England's muses
To animate our cheerless winter days.

Sweet minstrel of the woods! – whose raptures mingle
    In liquid notes between the moonbeams pale –
O that I yet may feel my pulses tingle
    At thy clear song. Be mine, before I fail,
To hear thy music in some darksome dingle
    And whisper, "Hark! It is the nightingale."

The Barefoot Maiden

A barefoot maiden, herding kye
    In a meadow near the mill,
Lay backward in the waving grass
To see the clouds in clusters pass
    Beyond the distant hill.
    Lifting a wistful eye,
She watched, o'erhead, the tangled mass
    Sweeping along the sky.

Away far up through azure deeps
    Like ships with sunlit sails
The clouds careered, each foamy crest
Bent forward in adventurous quest
    Sped by the summer gales.
    Split they the aery steeps
On, on toward the opening west
    Straining with sudden leaps.

'Twas as if she, a mermaid bright,
    Lay on the ocean bed,
Below the passing mariners
And keels of curious voyagers
    Which floated overhead.
    Dim shadows mixed with light
Were cast in little flickering stirs
    Down through the watery height.

Another fancy filled her mind,
    And lo! – A flock of sheep
Along Elysian fields were driven.
Their fleeces – white as souls new-shriven —
    From stains they sought to keep.
    A shepherd walked behind
    Urging them t'ward the folds of Heaven —
That shepherd was The Wind.

Up from the field, with burst of song
   A skylark took the wing.
   The dreaming maiden faintly heard
High in the heavens – not the bird,
   But an angel choir sing.
   All the evening long,
Sweetest music, she averred,
   Sang the celestial throng.

The sky flew past her upturned face
   Till she could almost feel
The spinning of this great round world
From whose equator clouds were hurled
   Like the dust of a chariot wheel.
   Vanished were time and place.
For lay she not on a star which whirled
   Far out through pathless space?

A merry heart the maiden bore,
   And though of humble birth,
Sang, near a tinkling waterfall,
A simple country madrigal
   To the beauty of the earth
The whole wide landscape o'er —
   Meadow and mill – she loved it all:
Shakespeare could do no more.

Sea Anemone

Thy tentacles wave to and fro
In search of prey
Treacherous yet beautiful
Anemone.

Acting
A living flower
But oh! What of the struggling prey
That's in thy power?

Rosa Excelsa

A rose is fairest on the prickly spray
   Where, with a somewhat sprightly freshness set
She joys in life and sunshine, till the grey
   Of pensive evening breathes a sweet regret.
But when the dainty flower, in gilded bowl
   No more by cool light winds of morn is tossed
Her simple pleasure to the ardent soul
   Half of its virtue and its worth has lost.
Where Nature placed her is she most possessed
   And most deserving of the studied praise
Of music-makers. Thus we love her best
   When, in her native haunts, a queen she stays:
For, winning fragrance on the breeze is flown,
While happy insects worship at her throne.

To a Sea-Gull

1

O Seabird, wild and free,
    With grey-plumed wings outspread!
Lord of the tempest-driven sea:
    Untamed and unafraid!
    With sudden beat and strong
    Thou sailest away on high,
Wheeling a lofty flight along the cloudy winter sky.

2

Fleet spirit of the gale!
    White-breasted, royal eyed.
Like musical note thy plaintive wail
    In the dance of the foaming tide.
    By salt-spray almost hid,
    Thou sweepest from out the steep:
Mingling an eerie cry amid the thunders of the deep.

3

Not as the mavis mild
    Upreared in leafy wood,
Cradled in freedom, thou the child
    Of wilder solitude,
    Thy home the rock unhewn
    Where heaving billows crack:
Thy nest the narrow ledges strewn with withered
                              ocean-wrack.

4

Thine is the broom-clad heath,
   Tall sea-cliffs, scarred and riven;
The whirling winds, and all beneath
   The canopy of heaven.
   With equal grace can thou
   Patrol the sandy bay,
Or plunge beneath the waves or bow thy neck and fly away.

5

O sea-mew! Calmly drift
   Beneath the morning sun;
Skimming the waters blue, where swift
   The living ripples run.
   Over the fitful sea
   With shadowing wings preside,
Crowned with a native majesty – the angel of the tide!

On the Breaking of the Moon
through the Clouds

With what a stately grace, serene and free,
    The moon divests herself of each soft cloud
    Which, with an ardent closeness, doth enshroud
The beauty of her pale austerity.
Supremely calm, she now unveils her face
    And with a somewhat sad aloofness leans,
    Diffusing shimm'ring brightness on those scenes
Below the compass of her height in space.

Charmed by the sheeny wonder of her light
    Round Cynthia still the grey clouds hover near
Too timid to approach the queen of night
    Yet loth to lose such pleasant, thrilling fear
And ah! On her unruffled brow the might
    Of lofty innocence now doth appear.

To a Speedwell

Wert thou a shining globe of dew
Hung in the evening air,
Where thou, reflecting Heaven's blue
Became a form so fair

That Beauty's presence in the land
Deemed thy cerulean dower
Too rare a gem to vanish, and
Preserved thee as a flower?

Thy dainty, shy, blue-petalled face
I spy upon the bank
Where it doth hold assertive grace
Among the grasses rank.

The discord of a fretting street
Will oft torment me less
Than thee, O Speedwell, with thy neat
Exquisite loveliness.

Thy keen sharp glance I understand.
Clear voice! I'll look above
The dusty road till I command
A source of purer love.

Thou speck of Heaven on earth, I dare
With faith's security
That we, with heavenly birth, should wear
A native purity.

Evening

The thankful voice of Nature, far and near,
   A vesper psalm is chanting lowliwise.
   From vale, field, hill, and rustic village rise
Faint undertones of music, swelling clear
To ripened praise – sweet, simple, strong, sincere.
   As in a cloistered minster slowly dies
   The choral service, so beneath these skies
And widening silence fills the atmosphere.

With flowing robe and flaming mitre dressed,
   God's minister, the sun, lifts holy hands
   In benediction on the waiting lands.
Awhile the world is one; but, being blest,
   Bird, beast and man arise. The flock disbands
Each to his kindred, seeking home and rest.

Cerithium

This finely-sculptured shell richly embossed —
Look you, what rare perfection of form
To be hidden in sand heaped with thousands more.
Why, why such shape be shattered wave-tossed,
Ground into grit such grace defaced by storm,
Beauty so slender-whorled whirled on the shore?

Hold, heart, hand on mouth – O cease!
Far out from land beyond the tide's leap
Slow architects, chasmed in purple peace,
Grope in dark forests, innumerable creep
             Fathoms deep.

Distance

I sat on a spur of rock,
And looked across…
There was the Jungfrau,
The Mönch, and the Eiger,
But a stone's toss.

Behind the mountain wall
With its peaks of snow
A full moon was rising
Coldly indifferent
As aeons ago.

Bird's-eye View

An early thrush with speckled breast
Sat brooding o'er her young,
Where, from a leaf-tip near her nest,
A shining dewdrop hung.

Her heart, such wealth to look upon,
Beat faster with delight —
Within the sparkling jewel shone
A rainbow on her sight.

So unto us, all unaware,
Like wonders come to pass,
When Nature in a moment rare
Lifts up her magic glass.

Spring Equinox

Again the great sea-mother, strength renewed,
Breaks her bonds, and now, with wild looks raging
And streaming locks, takes up the ancient feud,
    Old Terran in his fearsome den engaging.
Now foot by foot the conflict is pursued
    On sea and land, until, strong battle waging,
    She strikes her foe; his rampant pride assuaging,
She hurls him down fast-fettered and subdued.

Soon will the sun, her slave, as he comes dancing
    Down the hills, strew blossoms on the earth,
    And she, the great sea-mother, bring to birth
Her teeming hosts, with forms of life entrancing,
    While summer-long, in caverns green, the giant
    Turns in his sleep and mutters threats defiant.

Address to a Sea Anemone

Bees flit from flower to flower unharmed,
Immune from fear of deadly spells,
To suck sweet nectar from the bells;
And butterflies, by beauty charmed,
Flock near immortal asphodels.

But you salute your guests with guile,
And lovely petals interlaced.
You greet your victims with a smile —
A living blossom, double-faced,
With smooth attractive splendour graced.

The Palmist

Great mountain peaks beneath us, as we fly
Hold up their open hands. Look, far below,
Those knuckled fingers, groping in the sky
Wear diamond rings of gleaming ice and snow.
Their palms are scored with glaciers and the slow
Scars of old wounds, veined, too, with silver streams,
And cupped toward the mists that come and go
Like shadows of faint thought, in fleeting dreams.
Casting adown her eye in sudden gleams
The ancient moon her wrinkled face enshrouds.
She tracks a strange wild history there, it seems,
Riding her broomstick, peering from the clouds.
We, who annihilate Time, such things behold,
But who can tell the tale that there is told?

[The Skyline of Eternity]

In bold relief against the western sky
    Stands out the line of tempest-stricken trees.
Bare boughs and gnarlèd trunks unto the eye
    Take up their place in evening's sunset frieze.
Ne'er till tonight beheld I earth and heaven
    Each to the other blend as do they here
For winter hard – the veil of summer riven —
    Combines in one the distant and the near.

Thus when the rising winds of earth do shake
    The tender leaves of youthful ardour past
When in life's branches though the day is late
    The hidden plan of all appears at last
O may I then God's steadfast purpose see
Clear on the skyline of eternity.

[An Icy Breath upon the Window Blew]

With rare designs, the frosty air adorns
Our window panes, on chilly winter morns.
Artistic ferns, with finely feathered fronds,
Delight the eye, while memory responds
With thoughts of summer when our days possessed
The living leaves these lovely forms suggest.

A thousand stellar crystals we descry
All twinkling like the stars away on high,
Reminding us that every thought of love
Has its true origin in One above.
'Tis thus, by holy lives, the saints display
The virtues of their Lord from day to day.

When first – as silent as the falling dew –
An icy breath upon the window blew,
So that the frost began to crystallize
In wondrous fashion there before mine eyes,
No trace of order or of fair designs
Could I observe in such conflicting lines.

The countless beauties of the sacred page
Will oft-times thus the mind of faith engage.
At first these do but faint impressions make
As o'er the Word we meditation take.
Knowledge is formed of things both great and small
Yet lacks the secret bond uniting all.

But when the Spirit's breath prepares the mind,
Each line of truth more clearly is defined.
'Tis only then upon the waiting soul
All Scripture blends in one harmonious whole.
In fine proportion every part doth fit
True to itself and to all Holy Writ.

Daily Edition

Daily, a thousand years, the world's hand-press
Has punctually turned out editions new,
Yet with Time's sale the output grows, not less,
As hour by hour, a myriad shapes we view
Of bird and beast – letters cunningly set
By the great Compositor's skill, in sea
And earth and space; a strange bold alphabet
Of star, crab, butterfly, flower and tree;
Hieroglyphics of living flesh; lines
Of crystal; logarithmic curves of storm
And shell: harmonious symbols and signs
Bound fast, colour with colour, form with form.
    But we like children Nature's page peruse:
    We scan the type, but fail to read the news.

[**Not by Bread Alone**]

When we behold the morning clouds arise
    And fill with shining ranks heaven's wide expanse,
When nature's miracle repeats its first surprise,
    And the young lambs upon the meadows dance,
    Then must the heart, made glad, find utterance
In lyric rhapsodies, must shout and sing
    For joy; or, overcome, stand held in trance,
Swept by the joyous ecstasies of Spring.
The human spirit is a sensitive thing —
    A butterfly that flits from flower to flower
Or in the sun hangs lightly on the wing
    As if dissolved in joy for one brief hour.
Dull clerks, know this, men are not made of stone,
Nor spite of labour, live by bread alone.

To Myself I Say

"What mystic deep emotions pass o'er me,
When in the solitude of Nature's calm,
And free from this world's turmoil and alarm,
I listen to the murmur of the sea,
And standing on a lone and shelving rock
I watch the seabirds, screaming o'er the waves
Near yonder Brough, whose unexplorèd caves
Some deep and hidden secret seem to lock?
Can I explain this feeling which is mine
When scenes like these my willing heart enslave?

My only answer is, 'When standing on that rock
I worship Heaven's God at Nature's shrine'. "

The Purpose

Of those mild atmospherics which in us wake
    Ecstatic raptures, as the gentle breeze
To tremble with a quivering joy doth make
    The sunkissed leaves departing from the trees,
Would I instruct my timid muse, and hence,
    With eager feet, I venture far along
Inviting fields of untrod eloquence
    To catch the haunting echoes of a song.
Could I but catch the wistful note that thrills,
    Yet swift eludes the sense, my joy could plan
Such music as from earth, sky, sea and hills,
    Piercing the dullness of my flesh, would fan
The smould'ring spark of worship into fires
Of holy longings, undefined desires.

On a Prospect of Distant Hills

I am enamoured of the silent hills,
    Whose gently swelling eminences hide
Enchanted hollows, which my fancy fills
    With mossy nooks, where brooks contented glide.

On sunny days their pencilled outlines hold
    The homely touch of sight's familiar forms:
Should cold, grey mists their lonely tops enfold
    An upward yearning oft my soul there warms.

But chiefly for that quiet trust in God
    And disposition sweet, they give my mood,
Love I the hills. Though Conduct has not trod
    Desire's fondly cherished paths of good,

I to the hills will lift mine eyes at length
From whence I take a calm but joyous strength.

The Soul's Reply

"Set your affections on things above."

Delusive Sense! Why dost thou thus enquire
    If, in the regions of our future bliss
    These exultations we shall miss
Which here oft point us to that true Desire?
Such birds as love the spreading flood of light
    Which daybreak ushers in upon the air,
    Complain not that there is no starlight there
Informing their sweet notes of clear delight.

And shall the sons of day, when doth appear
    The shining fullness which He will display
Seek fretfully each lamp-like orb which here
    Afforded them a homeward guiding ray?
Stars are but meant for night, and serve to cheer
    Until the sure approach of brighter day.

Out of the Depths

"I will praise the Name of God with a song" – *Psalm 69. 30.*

"In my distress I called upon the Lord, and cried unto my God: He heard my voice out of His temple, and my cry came before Him, even into His ears. He sent from above, He took me, He drew me out of many waters." – *Psalm 18. 6, 16.*

Angelic voices, loud and clear,
    Their songs of worship ever raise,
That all creation's sons may hear
    The glory of Jehovah's praise.

Full many a sweet melodious chord
    Is struck from harps of purest gold,
Within that place where dwells the Lord,
    His great perfections to unfold.

Up to this holy temple came
    A cry raised out of waters strong
By one who trusted in the Name
    To whom salvation's acts belong.

The ear of God received the prayer,
    And full response was seen at length,
When, with His strong right arm made bare,
    The Lord came forth in saving strength.

Thick clouds of darkness 'neath His feet
    Concealed a path no man had trod.
The eye of faith alone could meet
    With footprints of the mighty God.

He rode upon a cherub bright,
    As forth on mercy's task He flew,
For love like His takes swifter flight
    Than e'er the wings of tempest knew.

The sinking man by Him was drawn
    From threatening wave, and waters deep;
His trembling foot was set upon
    A rock which storm-tides never sweep.

O precious thought that calms all fears!
    Our cries for help are heard by Him
Who daily in His temple hears
    The praises of the seraphim.

The Response

"What shall I render unto the Lord for all His benefits toward me?

"I will take the cup of salvation, and call upon the name of the Lord."
Psalm 116. 12, 13.

The sacred truth in David's song
 Has moved my soul yet once again.
A God in Heaven who waits so long
 To hear the sinful sons of men?

Yea! For the High and Holy One,
 Who from the purest glories came,
Declared that God, who gave the Son,
 Saves those who call upon His name.

Long years – alas – I've lain and slept
 At ease within self's lone estate,
Ne'er caring for the One who kept
 His patient watch without my gate.

Upon my darkened eyes there breaks
 The light of Calvary's solemn hour.
E'en now mine inmost soul awakes
 To know the love of God in power.

O woeful scene! The Saviour crowned
 With thorns, and by the world abhorred.
Men slay the Christ, in Whom was bound
 The promised mercy of the Lord.

No plea for mercy have I here,
  Save what, O Lord, Thyself doth give.
Thy grace invites me to come near
  To One on yonder cross and live.

Is this the God against whose laws
  Mine evil mind hath ever wrought —
The God whom I, without a cause,
  Would fain have cast from every thought?

I did not know Thee! O, my God,
  That e'er I could have spurned Thy Son.
Before the cross, with feet unshod,
  Amazed I stand. My heart is won.

To Thee, O God, my soul I lift
  In joyful unaffected praise.
Thanks be to Thee for love's great gift,
  Through life – through everlasting days.

"Whosoever shall call upon the name of the Lord shall be saved."
Romans 10, 13.

[Lengthen not the Inward Strife]

I know thine inmost soul has heard
My gentle voice of late
Why, since thy waking heart is stirred
Wilt thou have Me to wait?

'Tis I, thy Saviour, who through loss
My love for thee once proved
Canst thou behold Me on the cross
And still be all unmoved?

Turn not thy drooping eyes away
These sufferings were for thee
I died for you on that dark day
Yet turnest thou from Me?

O who on earth could be more dear
To thy now trembling heart?
An answer give in accents clear,
"Wouldst thou have Me depart?"

If thou but liftest up to Me
A cry for mercy here,
A Saviour's voice would set thee free
From every secret fear.

Dost thou not think Mine eye can trace
That thought to none made bare?
First come to Me for saving grace
Then roll on Me thy care.

With tender voice I ask once more
Thy halting, troubled heart,
"For ever from thy sin-closed door
Wouldst thou have Me depart?"

O lengthen not the inward strife
Thy soul at last to lose.
Between a swiftly passing life
And heaven's glories choose.

To Me who once to Calvary trod
A true response now make.
Lo! Here am I! Wilt thou from God
Me for thy Saviour take?

On Giving

Let not thy loving Master's watchful eyes
    Grow dim with grief, as He doth see thee sift
With pondered doubts and judgement too precise
    The measure of the calculated gift.
Be not as those, who from their nature's wealth
    Dole forth the pence, as they in deeds loud-cried,
Unlike the noble impulse done by stealth,
    Dispense such bounties with deliberate pride.
God gives not thus. No petty-natured laws
    Confine the limits of His love to man.
Reluctance knows Him not: or if He pause
    'Tis not to stint, but crown, His former plan.
So on the waters cast thy bread, nor mourn
For after many days it shall return.

Faith

The mariner, with straining sight,
Oft shielded by a wrinkled hand
Peers, by the fast-receding light
For glimpses of the distant land.

The sea-swept planks beneath his feet
Creak to the motion of the ship.
The elemental strife and sleet
Make him the wheel but firmer grip.

Why should the dark tumultuous main
By clear instinctive skill be met?
Believed he not that he would gain
A native port, unseen as yet?

Paul's Preaching

"Here stands the Cross! And here, the Sepulchre:
    Two mighty signs, God-given to every age.
    Hither, ye nations! – priest, barbarian, sage;
Assemble round, with royal spices, myrrh."
This herald of the risen Conqueror
    In his left hand holds high the Sacred Page,
    Raises his right an audience to engage —
Lo! Now he speaks, and all the crowd's astir.

"Jesus, the crucified, I here proclaim
    Son of the living God! Christ would I win
    Since on Damascus way revealed to me.
Not with a creed, but with Himself, He came.
    God's miracle – the sacrifice for sin.
    A prophet He? Nay more, the Prophecy!"

Paul in Prison

"Wert thou that youth, who from Gamaliel's hand
    The cup of Hebrew lore so deeply drained?
    Whose zeal against the Nazarene had stained,
With martyr's blood, Judea's lovely land?
Whence then this exile rude, this prison-band,
    From thwarted synagogue and rabbi gained?
    No crime 'gainst Rome? Why then with fetters chained,
In life-defence of Caesar's throne to stand?"

"A vision on Damascus way sufficed
    To blind my heart to all it treasured most;
        For HIM I saw, and lo! – my pride was quelled.
O fellow-prisoner! To be found in Christ
    Not all of ancient creed or private boast —
        Not life itself – have I too dearly held."

To an Engraving of Bishop Reynolds

Of choice engravings, framed upon the wall
   I chiefly love this bishop, grave and wise;
A preacher he who kept the creed of Paul,
   Nor winked at truth to favour royal eyes.
Much have I scanned of late the tufted beard,
   The tight round cowl, the mien of serious grace;
Each look I take, the more I hold revered
   This holy man with Virtue's modest face.

When pastor-guides, like Reynolds, tend the sheep
   Not less from love than weight of solemn charge,
The flocks of God are fed in pastures deep
   While crook and staff hold prowling wolves at large.
O well for England's church when men as these
Bear shepherd-rule in home or diocese.

Christ Risen

Up to the temple two disciples came;
    Yet e'er they passed within its gates to pray,
    Behold, upon the outer threshold lay
A lifelong beggar, destitute and lame.
Appeals for alms immediate audiences claim —
    For craving heaven, we meet not earth with nay —
    "Such as I have I give," did Cephas say,
"Rise up and walk in Christ of Nazareth's name."

Straightway the man by Peter's hand was raised
    In new-found strength to walk and leap between
The chosen two. With them he loudly praised
    Jehovah's mercy. Openly was seen
This miracle of note, and, all amazed,
    The multitude must own the Nazarene.

The Soul's Deliverance

Lines written after hearing a sermon preached on Psalm 40.

Athirst for living waters, I inquire
    If aught today as in this pew I sit,
    Shall lift my steps by prayer or Holy Writ
To firmer footing, far above the mire
Of sinking feeling. Heard is my desire,
    For lo, the preacher reads how from the pit
    King David was updrawn – words apposite
To souls from Sin's foul prison lifted higher.

What but the harp befits the ransomed hand?
    What but a song the mouth by God redeemed?
Here on the strong eternal Rock I stand
    With heart of laughter, as if I had dreamed
Of endless shades, but waked at the command
    Of One whose Saviour-name I'd else blasphemed.

The Miracle

"We must not send the multitude away
Hungry and travel-stained," the Saviour said:
    "Go ye, and let those fainting souls be fed."
"Lord, whence should *we* find food for these, I pray?"
Thus Philip spake: when Andrew swift did say,
    "Lo, here's a lad! With victuals husbanded.
    But – two small fish! Five loaves of barley bread! —
Master, among so many, what are they?"

"Bring them to Me!" The voice of One whose hand
    Dropped down the manna with the morning dew,
In ancient days, was sounding through the land.
    The loaves so little, and the fishes few,
Were blessed by Him, whose beautiful command
    The miracle of harvest wrought anew.

[Leaving Northbank]

No more with rhythmic step to sow the seed
Or thresh the grain on barn-floor or in loft
Now dispossessed I've quit my croft,
Sold it, and signed the deed.

No more I'll haunt the hill where once I flayed
My bank of peat or on the heather lay.
Mere relics now, I've put away
My tusker and my spade.

I had a farm-stead. Northbank was its name.
There life returned in ordered pace and near
To Nature's moods, as year to year
The punctual seasons came.

Now in a little cottage on the strand
I spend my days, musing upon the oracle,
Behind the old sea wall,
And there a deeper wisdom learn than that I found on land.

A Christian's Couplets in Time of War

Spake not, sayst thou, the ancient law of truth
"Sword meet with sword, take vengeance, tooth for tooth"?

Nay! But by the sad consent of Heaven
For your heart's hardness was the precept given.

Fight, fight ye, if ye must. But in your sinning
Remember 'twas not so in the beginning.

Take up the sword and hate with hatred face
But match not Moses' law with Heaven's grace.

Ah, was it so when in man's true defence
Goodness was crucified, at Love's expense?

Goodness sanction war? And did men draw the blade
That slayeth man in God's own Image made?

Should not a man, sayst thou, his lifeblood give
That so a fellow-countryman might live?

At whose cost, I ask, must blood be shed —
Thine own? Or from the life of silent foemen dead?

Princely Offerings

"The princes of Israel, heads of the house of their fathers ... brought their offering before the Lord."
[Numbers 7. 2–3]

"Leaders of each princely tribe,
Rise! and in rich gifts excel!
Substance, honour, wealth ascribe
To the God of Israel.
    See the congregation wait!
    Bring your offerings to the gate!"

Now the royal wagons come,
Bearing bowls of silver made,
Altar gifts, a goodly sum,
Silver chargers, duly weighed,
    Covered all with modest cloth —
    Right knows not what left hand doth.

Hark, the Lord His servant bids,
"Take it of them! Be it shared
'Mong the Levites – bullocks, kids,
Rams for sacrifice prepared,
    Flour fine, oil mingling well,
    Incense with a fragrant smell."

Most and last of all behold
Censer-spoons of shekels ten,
Fashioned each from purest gold
For the hands of priestly men.
    In the Sanctuary blest indeed
    Who in praise their brethren lead!

Between the Tidemarks

The legendary fight
(From Time's beginning fought)
Abates not day nor night.
Within the battle caught,
Between two worlds I go
In endless ebb and flow.

Because there are no rules,
I step from stone to stone
Across the little pools
That have so strangely grown,
Fed by invisible streams
Seen only in our dreams —

Until, past safe retreat,
I feel the advancing tide
Swirling round my feet,
And know in verity
That I, with all beside,
One with that world shall be.

The Floods Came

(31 January, 1953)

Along life's pleasant ayre
Between two worlds we go,
Caught within the snare
Of things familiar grown,
Nor heed the silent flow
Lapping rock and stone.

Against the great sea-wall
Which this from that divides
Beat mysterious tides,
Deep-ranked along the shore,
Until at last it fall
And time deceive no more.

The Ordeal

"They went both of them together."   *Genesis 22. 6.*

Into the gathering darkness
Between the thieves two
The Saviour enters inly
With One whom He knew:
"*Father*, forgive them —
They know not what they do."

With One whom He knew,
(Faithful to the end)
He drew His last breath
While the rocks rend.
"*Father*, to Thy hands
My spirit I commend."

The Chief Butler

Give me the cup: for I
Now a slave of His
Bear it (how years have flown!).
In fealty to One well-known,
Make obeisance to Him
Saviour of Egypt,
Lord on the throne.

Once, in prison I lay
Under the noose of death:
Into my dungeon He came,
Shared my sentence and shame,
Iron fetters wore,
Raised me to freedom —
Praised be His name!

The Riddle

Island with island joins in hand,
And I, by summer ritual led,
Within the magic circle stand.
They pass the ring from hand to hand,
Sunwise – though not a word is said.

I look across the narrow sound
To cliffs that front the western sea,
And ask if in their haunted ground
The golden ring perchance be found:
Each answers, "It is not in me."

The headlands hide a secret door
Foot cannot find nor hand unlock,
Yet as I roam upon the shore
I seek that hidden trove once more,
Fast held in obstinate rock.

Softly with measured ebb and flow
The ocean to itself repeats
The password given long ago,
And wave to wave, as it retreats,
Whispers what I can never know.

What lamp? What spell of Orient leaf
What Sesame of joy or grief
Will turn the lock that I may scan
Treasures which the turbaned thief
Has seized from Time's slow caravan?

But as I catch the gleam of gold,
Or open find the fabulous den,
The shining ring they all withhold,
And I in silence go again
Sleep-wandering through the world of men.

The Beautiful Feet

"How beautiful upon the mountains are the feet of Him that bringeth good tidings." Isaiah 52. 7.

Awake, awake! – gone are the days of mourning!
    By eager fingers let those harps be strung
    So long on Babylonian willows hung.
Arise! go forth with singing! and returning,
Shake off the dust of exile. Up, arise!
    On Zion's hill your God and Saviour reigneth
    And by His might each hostile arm restraineth.
Let songs of gladness drown your doleful sighs.
Hark how a voice upraised in exultation,
    Echoes the joyful news from hill to hill.
    Run forth in welcome, hands outspread to fill
With princely gifts those hands that bring salvation,
    And on His way Heaven's Royal Envoy meet,
    Fall down amazed, and clasp those wounded feet.

On the Cross

Psalm 118. I Corinthians 15

Hell's angry hive was there,
Round them like swarming bees.
Upon a cross He hung,
Compassed by enemies
On every side.
They stung Him till He died.

Sin's sharpest deepest thrust
He there in silence bore,
But conquered at the last,
His bitter sufferings o'er.
Now *we* can sing,
"O death, where is thy sting?"

Gifts and Glory

When the Lord came down to earth
There was music, there was mirth —
Angels singing in the sky
"Glory be to God on high."
    Let us, too, rejoice and sing
    Praises to our Saviour-King.

When the Lord came down to earth
There were riches, there was worth.
Treasure chests with wealth unpriced
Opened to the infant Christ —
    Gifts of myrrh, frankincense, gold
    Can we our small mite withhold?

On that holy Christmas night
There was glory, there was light.
Through the midnight shone the star
Guiding wise men from afar
    Till the Saviour they could view.
    Grant that we may find Him too.

One Flock

John 10.16

"Other sheep I have,
Scattered far away —
Lambs for which I died,
    Now to wolves a prey.

"These, too, I must bring:
    This My Father's will.
I, through you, would seek
    These, my lost ones, still.

"They shall hear My voice,
    Calling them by name,
And shall follow Me,
    Though but weak and lame.

"There shall be one flock,
    Holy, safe and fair,
Gathered from the hills
    By the Shepherd's care."

One great Shepherd then
    In their midst shall be,
Loved by all the flock,
    Praised eternally.

The Shepherd's Soliloquy

What was that vision? What that sight,
Which from us now is gone?
Was it indeed the Lord's own light
That lately on us shone?
Whose songs were those which told
Of Saviour born? – though first we feared!
Angels they were, such as appeared
To Abraham of old.

They waited – but only the stars looked down
And all within their sight
Was the dark hillside and distant town
In the silence of the night.
Yet jubilant they sped:
"O hasten, and before Him fall
Good tidings of great joy to all,"
Was what the angel said.

They listened – but now was naught to hear
Save bleating of the sheep
And in the still night atmosphere
Faint sighs of things asleep
And a soft rustling in the grass.
"Come let us go," they said, "that we
May for ourselves in Bethlehem see
This that has come to pass."

[**Community**]

This shall ye ne'er forget, beloved, when breaking
This one whole loaf, and from one cup partaking,
    Members are ye of Christ and one another,
    Brother with brother.

When we together dwell, one God adoring,
Strengthening the feeble and the weak restoring,
    Then that last holy precept gently spoken
    We keep unbroken.

Lord, unto this Thy love shall make us willing:
Thou wilt Thyself in us this grace fulfilling,
    Bring home one flock, Thyself, one Shepherd guiding,
    All good providing.

Rackwick, Hoy

'Twas Lord's Day. And, to meditation given,
    I walked in solitude the winter shore,
    Where even Nature's wildest moods restore
Slow tranquil thought. The sea-waves, landward driven,
Tossing their plumes like knights for battle shriven,
    Rank upon rank, with deep and sullen roar
    Urged on their steeds, and great cloud-banners bore
Flung to the wind, in angry tatters riven.

And then beside the mouth of rocky caves
    I read the ancient words of David's Psalm,
      "The floods, O Lord, have lifted up their voice:
Thou, Thou alone, canst make the storm a calm".
      And shouted to the earth, "Rejoice, rejoice,
The Lord is mightier than the mighty waves".

A Disciple Speaks

Within these parchments, oft transcribed,
Long did the fathers of our race
Seek out a mystery whose depth
The very angels seek to trace.

Line upon line, they followed clues
Concealed in prophecy and psalm,
And in strange codes and riddles dark
Read a celestial cryptogram.

But who could give the countersign?
Whose skill unseal the sacred roll?
Or find the cipher that unlocked
The hidden message of the whole?

To Him who is the Living Word
Blessing and praise for ever be! —
Our eyes beheld a glory once
Which kings and prophets longed to see.

And now, in law and chronicle,
With burning hearts, His steps we trace;
For there His moving shadow falls,
Since first we looked upon His face.

We heard Him speak, we watched Him die,
With whom we walked in Galilee.
Again we read the ancient scroll,
And cry aloud, "'Tis He! 'Tis He!"

The Imperishable Thing

O say not Beauty dies unsung!
    The passing cloud, the morning star,
The daffodil with dewdrops hung,
All lovely transient things and young
    Somewhere remembered are.

It may be quiring angels need
    A sweetly blended music-score,
And in the forms of beauty read
Fair notes, and thus from pipe and reed
    Divinest music pour.

What though the loveliness of things
    Be from Time's changing book erased,
That's lost not which an Angel sings;
What matters Nature's scatterings
    If only God be praised?

Then mourn not, Poet, if thou fail
    To read the subtle notes aright!
Thou, too, wilt at the last prevail.
Love practiseth the heavenly scale
    For the far choirs of light.

Lord and Christ

He is not here, but is risen again!
An angel of dazzling brightness
Sits upon the sepulchre
In vesture of snowy whiteness.
Empty and tenantless the tomb
Burst are the bars of the prison.
Victory! Christ is risen:
Alive again is He.

[Praise Be to Him]

Praise be to Him who saw our hapless plight
Where sin's dread reef loomed black against the skies
And in His pity heard our urgent cries.
Let thankful songs of praise to Him arise
Who for our rescue dared Golgotha's night
And on the waters launched Heaven's high emprize.

Swift as the tide that rolls
In foaming strength between our island shores
And breaks in foam on hidden shoals
Rode down into the storm to save our souls
Salvation's mighty Captain from on high.

Home Thoughts

This Christmastide, as round the fire you stoop,
    To muse on life's fast-woven woof and warp,
The vacant places in the family group
    May touch responsive chords on memory's harp.
Within Reflection's silent pool we see
    The fabled towers and castles of the past,
But let no earth-born wind the image free
    In ruffled surface of the lake at last.
The melodies of former years still sound
    Far sweeter echoes, through the vaults of time.
The unformed joys of childhood yet are found
    By distance moulded perfect and sublime.
And then! Faith tells us of a home above
Where tears ne'er dim the sacred eye of love.

The Pirate's Grave

A shipwrecked pirate lad was he
    Who now no peaceful trader kills.
He that chased others o'er the sea,
    Was chased and buried in the hills.

The Yacht Sings

The yacht sings, and with white wings outspread
Leaps over the waves. The bubbling wake
Reckless with joy writes its chronicle
In dancing foam, and our small white boat
Glides on. In this magic hour mind
And imagination draw to themselves
New sense of beauty in sun and sky.
Sea and islands mingle in delight,
The bright horizon bounding all. Tide
And wind wrestle, and with flashing spray
Sprinkle the ocean. We, too, are seized
In a wild happiness and a mood
Of strange freedom and release.

The Boy and the Daisy

He stood within the little field,
And in his hand he held the sun.
Its tips of flame around him flew:
He plucked the petals one by one.
A miracle was there concealed —
And bright his eyes with wonder grew.

Then as he broke the hollow cone
That streamed and ran with golden heat,
The winged Promethean fire had flown,
And all its wealth to ashes turned.
But flowering thickly round his feet,
A thousand worlds in splendour burned.

[Apocalypse]

In a single night the mushroom rose
And underneath it the black gnomes
Danced in the air as the castles fell down
Dust on a thousand homes.

Exiled on a planet shore, a man
Wide-eyed with terror marks
At each hammer-stroke the starry constellations
Scatter like anvil sparks.

Dream Procession

In an hospital bed
I lie with pillowed head
And watch upon the wall
Pale reflections fall
     Of ritual moving shapes
     Whose phantom shade escapes
     From lighted corridor
     In through the open door
     And as they come and go
     I feel the silent flow
     Of unseen presences
     Ordained to heal and bless,
     And on my hospital bed
     Am strangely comforted.

Convalescence

In a private world of their own
Of wild-winged ecstasies
Blackbirds and busy sparrows
Here disport, where vision narrows
To a green hospital lawn
Cloistered by screen of trees.

In sick-ward long confined
To me are now restored
Things gone quite out of mind —
The joy of summer's wealth —
And through my body poured
The glow of inward health.

O happy happy world
Where sunlight with its rays
Silvers the verdant earth,
Where song-birds sing their praise
And I again am thirled
To summer and its mirth.

As a Boy in a Field

I stood in a little field,
A daisy in my hand
And wondered what lay concealed
In a thing so perfectly planned.

I plucked with finger and thumb
The petals one by one
And saw their image become
A metaphor of the sun.

I broke the flaming cone
But nothing at all was there
But a green lining lightly thrown
Around invisible air.

On a London Street

1932

Faded flowers in fist,
A chain of slum children —
From summer fields long missed.

Not now can squalor stain
The pure bright image
Of that fair green domain.

In mute defiance
Young eyes have glimpsed
God's glory in dandelions.

His miracle of leaf and blade,
Bud and blossom,
All that He has made.

The Peat Worker

With toiling hands and patient shoulder bent
Awhile he paused and on his tusker leant.

The Poet

I met the other afternoon
A poet, who's a Kirkwall loon.

He raved about the billows wet;
His deep sea music haunts me yet.

His hands, which dash off daily screeds,
Are apt to tremble as he reads.

A deep disgust of socks and ties,
Long looked at, filled that poet's eyes.

He moved about upon the loch
Like a nimble Dutchman by Van Gogh.

And wore, with aspect most remote,
Big waders and an oilskin coat.

The Sea-Wall

This is the old sea-wall, lichened with age.
Here it stands, fixing a frontier line
To shield Time's wealth against the implacable sea.
Behind it lie men's labours – farm and field,
Castle and mart, green garth and populous town,
And all the multitudinous roads that cross
The world's wide plain...
                   Beyond it, ringed in light,
Crouches the vast and hollow-sounding sea.
               *

See them – these huge blocks, lifted and laid
By strong ancestral arms; great corner-stones,
Fluted and tooled; with strange old masonry
Dug up from ruined long-lost palaces;
Slabs of worn roofs; and from the churchyard loam
Tombs of the dead, despoiled by Time's slow hand.
Not these alone, but from the grey stone wave
That curls its crest with unrelenting rage
Up to its grassy verge in verdant foam,
Savage rock-boulders, which primeval hands,
Long centuries ago, set in their place,
And which destroying years have oft pulled down,
But man's proud faith restored, built and rebuilt.
               *

Some few there were who lived upon the shore,
Scorning retreat, and looked upon the sea
With patient wary eyes, reaping the spoils
Of storm and tide – chance bits of timbered wood,
Masts of old ships, and flotsam of the deep —
Or finding curious amulets from distant lands,
Brown beans and spotted nuts, and now and then

A rare unusual shell. They knew each rock,
Each inlet where the shoals of fishes come,
Each cave and cliff, each weed-hung cranny where
The great crab finds retreat; the seasons, too,
When all the migrants of the teeming shore
Seek seaward, or return among the pools.
Yet in the evening when the smiling sun descends
And the burning West with ritual calm
Fulfils her sacred mystery, these turn
To gaze with distant eyes toward the West
As if another world they sought lay hidden there.

*

I too, like these, in vague fantastic worlds
Within the wall's confines have lived and toiled,
And wandered there disconsolate and confused
Among the darkening hills, to deeper gloom.
Familiar things there unfamiliar turned
And darkness burned with ghostly flame.
True became false, and what was certain dark.
The people walked and shouted in their dreams,
And waved their arms, yet all was still as night.
It was a strange and unexpected land.
Yet through the hours and days and months and years
Moments would chance, when I again would be
Half-comforted by sense of what had been
In some lost other world, gone in despair
But only half-forgot. And I would say,
I have not always here in darkness been,
And that lost other world may yet regain.

The Mast

Landward is tossed
The broken mast,
Its pride of sail
All stripped and gone,
Blown to the skies
By winter gale
And left at last
With not a stitch
Of canvas on.
It felt the good ship
Plunge and pitch
As she the wide
Atlantic crossed
And loved to rise
Among the stars
Or wildly dip
With sudden swing
To shake the spray
From ropes and spars…

Two-year-old

The Coalman

Look, Auntie! – I am the coalman.
This cushion on my back
Is a great big sack.

Tell me, Auntie, where shall I put it?
It's ever so heavy to carry
To the house from the lorry.

See, I'll put it down on the mat
By this old easy chair;
It'll do fine there.

There is a note with the weight
Showing what you are due —
Six pennies will do.

Four Bells

"All hands, lash up, LASH UP! Lash up and stow!"
    The old ship-chaunty's raucous cry is breaking
    The 'forrid' mess deck's slumber, and rudely now awaking
The tardy sleepers in the flat below.
Rings out again that call. "Hello! Hello!
    Rouse up here – you! – without another shaking:
    Else it'll be the 'rattle' for ye, no mistaking.
Four bells have gone, young fellow, don't y' know?"

I swing to the deck, lash up, and, though on duty,
Beside the after casement 'swing the lead'.
    The slowly-rising sun, in solemn beauty
    Out of his cloudy hammock lifts his head —
And *still* he's shouting, "Come along, my hearties,
Cook, stokers, steamboat-crews, and working parties."

The Return from Innisfree

I will arise and go now, and go to London town,
And a tall attic take there, with dusty window-panes:
Poor neighbours will I have there, with beggars
                                broken-down,
And trudge with tramps in the back-street lanes.

And I shall breathe grey smoke there, for smoke
                              comes swirling low,
Down from the factory chimneys to where
                              a woman sings;
There the midnight's an inferno, and the moon
                              a painted show
Of life's unimaginable things.

I will arise and go now, for dreams of old romance
Lead but to Life's desertion beyond the city's roar;
So when I walk the pavement and seek the truth,
                               perchance
I'll find it through a slum's dark door.

The Tragedy

Rising in foam-crested breakers, O Western Ocean,
what ailed thee?
What pain or what anger was thine that with
landward-thundering roll
Thou lifted thy strength, and not from the
canvas-rigged vessels that sailed thee,
But here from a rock on the shore, demanded thy
pitiless toll?

Calmly thou driftest today; yet I fear thee, for oh,
I remember
The stealthy incoming wave, and the treacherous deed
that was done.
More evil by far, I esteem, than the howling gales of
November
Those surges that swept the ledge bare, 'neath a wintry
smile from the sun.

Art thou a god then, neglected, but claiming from all
who would ride on
These waters so wide, or wander the shore-line,
an offering, O Sea?
Were the old fishers of Greece who devoted their nets
to Poseidon,
Imploring his favour when venturing seaward, more
pious than we?

Vainly, O Western Ocean, thou vauntest. Ah no, not
                                                    for ever
Shall the bones of these innocent victims in
                              weed-haunted caverns be kept.
The ancient decree shall stand fast, that the Sea her
                                        dead must deliver
And the Ocean be widowed one day for the sake of the
                                        widows that wept.

[Colosseum]

Behold the great arena, round whose space
The towering walls rise heavenward, tier on tier,
Upon its stance the athletes now appear,
(Poised on the line, and stripped to run the race)
Encompassed by the eager populace.
Eye fixed upon the prize, they persevere
With hand outstretched, until in full career
The foremost gains the mark and slacks his pace.

Imperial trumpets in salute are blown,
And as the victor, to their joyful sound,
Is led in triumph up to Caesar's throne,
There to receive the trophy, his by right,
The cloud breaks into thunder – height to height
Echoes with wild applause while he is crowned.

[The Dim-Seen Goal]

Ambitious boy! A poet would'st thou be?
Since such thy heart desires, then learn from me
A poet's temperament, and noble soul.
If thou must press toward the dim-seen goal
Then know the elevated plane of thought
In which thy Muse should tread. Thus taught,
By rising higher, thou shalt then descend
To fellow-feeling with thy fellow men.

Dig, Dig those Daisies

Go
Dig, dig those daisies from the lawn
Grass is the thing to tread upon
Cut down those dandelions bright
We have no wish to take delight
O'er such intruder sent by heaven —
With grass seeds costing six and seven
Let Nature's bounty be withdrawn
Dig, dig those daisies from the lawn.

The Reef

Stormed at by wind and tide
Its front defies the foe;
Besieged on every side
Dark rocks repel each blow
And with determination
Keep steadfast hold on stance and station.

Innocent of rude assault
The long dark slope, foam-flecked,
Is doomed to bear the fault
Of fair vessel wrecked
That on it long has wintered
Mast gone, and timbers splintered.

Rock-ledges, arms outflung
Lean seaward and creviced caves
By tangle-weed o'erhung
Give shelter from the waves,
The slanted roof, unyielding,
A thousand small sea-creatures shielding.

Amid leap, lash, and splash
Of landward-surging seas
That on its ledges crash
The reef remains at ease,
Making no rude commotion.
It rises calm and dauntless from the ocean.

Life

Morning to evening, 'mid the moving crowds
    The city's toilers wrought.
Morning till night – blue skies and fleecy clouds
    But man perceived it not.

Evening to morning – gaiety and sleep,
    Though lovely is the night
And twinkling stars their ancient watches keep,
    Untroubled, calm, and white.

Morning to eve, one worker now and then
    Looked upward with a sigh,
And, by the King of Heaven's decree, again
    The white clouds floated by.

Evening to morning – a quiet glance took he
    Up to the Milky Way,
Lay down and slept, and sleeping, wandered free
    The dreamlands of the day.

Frolic in the Stratosphere

I saw old Sol, the Sailorman, dive
    From the top of the world's main-mast,
And the jolly fellow, as I'm alive,
        Upward a splash directed
        So merry and unexpected,
        That the stars rushed out aghast.

Only the pale Steersman of the night,
    As he kept his watch by the wheel,
Smiled at the fo'c'sl's stupid fright;
        With one eye broadly winking
        Looked he upon me, thinking
        Of the Captain under the keel.

The stars, excited to a man
    Sprang for the upper deck,
Grew pale, and up the rigging ran;
        Then hung with great eyes bulging
        Over a sea divulging
        No secret by foam or fleck.

"Drowned," said they, "as we foresaw,
    But his death's to be deplored!"
When up came Sol with a huge guffaw,
        On the far side re-appearing:
        The pale moon left off steering
        As the Captain climbed aboard.

At this the young stars, sorely shamed,
    Back to their cabins crept,
While the merry old Sailorman Sol exclaimed,
        "Who spy upon their betters
        Had best be clapt in fetters,
        And in their places kept."

Premonition

The guttering dip
In the chandelier
Expired in a flame,
Ghostly and clear —
And the tall young candles
Melted with fear.

Through the forest rang
The woodman's blade.
Low on the ground
The oak was laid —
And the young green saplings
Shivered and swayed.

The funeral passed
Through the narrow street,
Black coffin, and men
With slow-paced feet —
And the children hushed
At their hearts' quick beat.

The Devil's Thimble

Touch it not – the bad man's thimble
Redd'ning on the heath
Squinting goblins, more than one,
    Lurking underneath
Snap in glee their fingers nimble
    At th'unwary child.
To thy little comrades run;
    Be not thou beguiled.

Green and purple, blue and yellow
    Will they pinch thine arm
Round thy hair like buzzing bees
    Wildly will they swarm,
Startle thee with sudden bellow
    Coming from behind?
Climbers round thee climb and squeeze
    Whensoe'er inclined.

Lift away thy curious finger
    From the baneful weed
Of an evil thing before thee
    None will give thee heed.
O my darling, do not linger
    Idly sulking, so —
Should the little black men call thee
    Thou with them must go.

Then twice twenty hands will grip thee
    Toss thee in the air
Sting thy cheeks with burning nettles
    Pluck thee by the hair
Then wilt fall, when they shall trip thee,
    With a sick'ning thud
Spilling like the flower's petals
    Drops of redd'ning blood.

Come, my child, before enchanted
    Leave the pretty flower.
See, the children are at play.
    O'er the grass they scour.
Hark! They call thee, thou art wanted.
    In the field they wait.
    Why so dreamy-eyed today?
    Ah! Too late! Too late.

Winter

Vanished the vernal
    Joy that was Spring's.
Remains but the kernel.
The true and eternal
    Inscrutable things
Existence – and Death
    With his shadowing wings.

Darkness, the sources
    Of Life and of Birth
The Stars in the courses,
    The Ocean-pent forces
That circle the earth
These with their sadness
    Chasten our mirth.

Powers primeval
    Stir in my breast.
In strange wild upheaval
Virtue and evil
    Rise to the test
Of issues immortal
    By Winter exprest.

Vain the devices
    Which blossomed in May.
The sweet summer spices
Whose fragrance entices
    Our manhood away —
Winter reminds us
    "Cold is the clay."

[Things that Could not Be]

Thrice have I seen the solid earth dissolve
And in a timeless moment felt
Rocks and mountains melt
In insubstantial air.
Once in a legendary cave
The grey sky fell.
It was beside the ocean, and I saw
Mingling sun and stone and wave,
The great world's atoms whirl and revolve,
Form and re-form,
Hither and thither tossed
In wind and light and storm,
Time's ancient law
Confused and lost
Of then and now, of here and there…
But how it chanced I cannot tell.

Nor can I tell
How things that could not be, befell
One certain day in summer long ago.
A cliff was there,
Vertical from the sea, and precipiced
Tier on tier to the hill,
And far below
Beat, like an oracle, the huge Atlantic surge.
But in an instant sight and sound were changed.
The hillside sloped
Up to the clouds and groped
For lost familiar sun and moon and stars.
I thought that I had reached the utmost verge
Of time and space or burst the invisible bars

That guard the secret exit none have known
And, from the earth estranged,
I wandered within a land remote and still,
If east or west
Or if in vanished time or time to come
I did not know.
And how to find return I did not know
From that strange place,
Whether by former landmarks still
I might my steps retrace,
Regain the ancient track along the hill,
Or would for ever roam
In timeless space,
Away from home, and yet at home.

Midsummer Night

On this midsummer night are spells unbound
From all inanimate things; as we stray
Beside the margin of this northern bay
Weird motions fill the air, till sight and sound
Confused, tremble with joy, and thought confound.

The rocks, transfigured, change from dark to bright,
The islands soar aloft in ecstasy,
And the great cliffs which tower from the sea,
Uprooted from their place, dissolve in light,
Fly from us, and are gone beyond our sight.

And ocean waves with deep orchestral roar
Mingle in prelude with the wind's wild notes.
Higher, and higher still, the music floats,
Till we at last are left upon the shore,
Listening for things that can be heard no more.

All now that sense can touch or see or hear
In swift abysmal floods of light have spanned
The invisible bounds, and we as exiles stand
Dumb and resigned, while o'er that strange frontier
Familiar forms like phantoms disappear.

The moment fades. Again on sea and shore
Old shapes return, and nothing meets our sight
Save the familiar rocks, and the waves breaking white,
Yet these have signs become of something more
Than what they in themselves had been before.

A Little Hillside Lane

I know a little hillside lane
    With ditch of golden furze
Where blackbirds build and trailing flowers enchain
    Thorns of the ancient curse.

There under intertwining stems
    The piping linnets dart
There, too, the daisies lift their diadems
    Glad'ning the wanderer's heart.

Between the moorland and the ditch
    Rises an old hill-dyke
Topped by a crazy fence the wires of which
    Have many a fleece-hung spike.

'Tis but two years since first I found
    This unfrequented track
And now that summer's here, to that loved ground
    I'll sometime wander back.

The Brocken

1

A weird dim spectre oft has been,
'Tis said, on lone Hartz mountains seen,
    Up where a tower stands
    On lofty pasturelands.

The shepherd and his sheep, the tower,
Are sometimes in a magic hour
    Against the clouds in vast
    Gigantic shadows cast.

'Twixt heaven and earth Titanic forms
Walk, with their shoulders in the storms:
    Upon the mountains wet
    Their strong firm steps are set.

The gaping goat-herd wonders why
The gods are wandering through the sky,
    And fain would he divine
    The import of the sign.

The low sun sinks – the phantom's fled,
And, like the unremembered dead,
    Is vanished into naught,
    Vanished and quite forgot.

2

The ancient Greeks and Romans sought
Life's joy where gladiators fought
  Until the arena ran
  With blood of beast and man.

Swift-footed were they in the chase
And swiftly from the arrow-case
  Could fill Diana's bow
  Against the panting doe.

Though wide the world, the human mind,
More ample still, must unconfined,
  Vision upon the skies
  Dramas which earth denies.

Old warriors heard the clash of shields
And chariots, in th' Olympian fields:
  Huge thunder-bolts saw hurled
  Flaming against the world.

"The gods are warring in the skies,"
Said they, "and when a hero dies,
  Along the clouds is shed
  His life-blood, flowing red."

A Cliff Conversation

"Lie down and look over
The cliff-top with me:
A selkie is swimming
Down there in the sea.
Wild fulmars are skimming
The tops of the waves,
And white breakers cover
The mouth of the caves.
There are four Tammy-Norries
Set there on that ledge,
And thousands of scorries..."
      "Boy, come back from the edge!"

"With menacing motion
Where the water is dark
Glides out on the ocean
A huge basking shark.
To capture a fish
A scarfie dives low.
Gulls swoop with such very
Fine grace to and fro.
Around yon black skerry
Foam lies like white lace,
And oh, I could wish..."
      "Boy, keep back from the face!"

On Boardhouse Loch

Idly afloat one summer day
On Boardhouse in my little boat
I sought the beach and all alone
Landing on the loch's far shore
I stepped with care from stone to stone,
And found a convocation there
Of full nineteen wild flowers or more
Arrayed in silken robes of green
(But how it happened who can say)
Their clustered heads of blues and yellows
Of white and purple, pinks and reds
Brought there together by occult charm
Or unseen spell of wind or weather
These spectral guests from field and farm
And moorland hill to join their fellows.

Never can fade from my delight
This fair community of flowers
That in so small a space
Showed such diversity and grace.
I felt abashed
Then with hushed breath tiptoed away
And waded to my little boat.
When on the water well afloat
I looked round there again
That fair community of flowers.

[**Ocean and Reef**]

Out from the geo we man this little skiff
Toward the perilous verge where interlock
Ocean and reef beside a beanstalk cliff
Whose menacing height looks down upon the shock
Of swirling tides that flood the shining rock.
From ledges overhead and mouth of caves
The guardian ranks of guillemot and auk
Recite dark incantation to the waves.

Imitations

Fly away, pretty moth,
     Fly away!
     If you stay,
Some boy, by my troth,
     Will come with a net
     And capture you yet.
     Fly away!

Sparrow, perched upon the tree,
One wise thing thou teachest me —
     Only birds that lightly cling
     To the earth can chirp or sing.
So may I hold by a spray
This poor world – then fly away.

The Flood-Tide

Beyond its wonted height, floods on the tide,
    Till beach and quay o'er-lapped with water are.
    Along the roadway drifts a floating spar —
No hand can stay the waves' insistent pride.
Beside the harbour-gate, where salts abide,
    Speaks out, in deep-set voice, an aged tar,
    "'Tis but a flowing storm-wash from afar;
A spent Atlantic gale, with breakers wide."

Across the soul of man, there oft will sweep
    Strong mystic floods, outborne from Life's broad sea —
The rising surge of instinct, swift and deep;
    A hallowed thought, an inward agony.
O Man. Awake! Thy very passions keep
    Dim intimations of Eternity.

Sea Symphony

I

Stone-deaf,
The old grey cliff
Leans seaward
Her dull-lit caves,
Dark and dolesome-wet —
Dead auricles,
That hear not and speak not,
But reverberate loud nothingness
In dumb echoes,
Dim echoes,
Echoes . . .

Their dark recesses,
Time-hollowed
Into deep clefts,
And hallowed grave sea-music,
Make muted moan,
As old Ocean,
Vexed and torn
With restless passionate tides,
Racked on the ribs
Of timbered ships,
And fretted with foam,
Lays his lips
Against her sense-dulled ear,
And, trumpet-clear,
With mighty voice resounding from the rocks,
Unlocks
His ancient store
Of legendary lore.

The foam-flecked billows,
Bellowing
And thundering,
Awaken the crying sea-birds
That flock and flit in the mouth of the caves
Like feathered memories,
And strike sub-conscious harmonies,
As those first stirred
In a poet's mind —
Half-spoken, half-heard,
Past thought, past word —
Images undefined
Of unimaginable excellence
That stutter and stammer forth
The incipient sense
In broken rhyme
And rhythms bravely rude.

In gales
Of urgent speech
He now recalls
And tells
Wild Scandinavian tales . . .
Of Nuckelavee,
That dread sea-demon.
Human-headed,
Horse-limbed,
Framed in huge proportions,
With sinews that twine and twitch
With serpentine contortions,
And Cyclopean eye,
Flame-shot,
Red-rimmed,

Body raw-fleshed
Meshed with veins
Where dragon's blood
Bubbles and boils —
A black flood
Of molten pitch,
Drained and drawn
From the heart's cauldron...
Of the maiden-devouring
Mester Stoor Worm
Slain by Assipattle...
Of mermaids forsaken
That haunt the desolate holms,
Of the ancient fugitive Wrekin...
Tales of that phantom ship
Whose tall foretop
Rakes the moon...
Weird songs
Of Trows and Selkies
And fabulous Fin Folk...
The lost legends
Of the great Sea-mother,
And of angry Terran
Fettered on the dungeon-floor
Of the utmost deep...
Till the old grey cliff,
Crazed with sound,
Nor hears nor speaks,
But casts back
Inarticulate cries
Into the great Void.

II

Now is the Vore-tullye,
Season of tempest,
When, battle-bent,
The long sea-breakers,
Tossing their snowy plumes
In middle air,
Sweep landward, fury-driven,
Sharp lances lower,
And, rank on rank,
With deep and sullen roar
Urge on their steeds,
And great cloud-banners bear
Flung to the wind,
In angry tatters riven.

But, winter gone,
War yields to armistice,
And o'er Old Ocean's
Wrinkled face
Mild emotions
In gentle ripples run —
Murmuring, whispering, rustling,
Ever dissolving, re-forming,
Changing and jostling
In intricate rhythmical measures,
Advancing,
Retreating,
Ruffling and dancing...
Responsive to each vagrant mood
Of summer's bright solicitude.

Aware,
In his vast solitudes,
Of all things that have been
Since Time began,
He sits and broods...
Recovering with infinite patience
The slow insistent murmur
Of distant generations;
Across his brow's majestic span
Serenely float
Great tranquil pools of thought —
Mirrors,
On whose bright surface glassed
Cloudy memories cumulate
From the inaccessible past,
And faint episodes,
Refracted on the mind's angle
From age to age,
Stand re-enacted.
Again his eye surveys
In visions dim
Voyages
Beyond the edge
Of the world's rim —
Stout dragon vessels sailing forth,
All manned by sea-kings of the north,
Deeds done, strokes essayed,
Risks run, kingdoms made.

Now one by one,
In his reflective calm,
Heroic names
(Like starry constellations

In Fame's
High firmament)
Take up their stations:
Sigurd the Stout,
Thorfinn the Mighty,
Einar, Paul;
Harald Hardrada,
Erlend, Olaf,
Hakon, Kol,
Earl Rognvald, saint,
Earl Magnus, martyr,
In Egilsay slain;
Asmund and Erling,
Thorkill and Eindrid,
Sigmund, Sweyn.

III

Summer-sensitive,
And touched with recollective thought,
Ocean breaks into music —
Muffled, melodious,
Nigh inaudible,
Till, gathering strength,
The long sea-dirges
Re-echo among the caves,
Where white gulls,
Ghostly-winged,
Swoop down from the grey ledges,
Screaming and wailing,
Perpetually calling,

Ye waves that meet
Where strong tides surge,
Go drum the dirge
Of proud defeat
O'er Hacon's fleet.

Ships full six-score
At anchor lay.
War-shields they bore
In ranked array,
And banners gay.

Death comes, alas,
On raven-wings,
And even kings
Like shadows pass
From mortal things.

The sun's eclipse
With sudden gloom
And pallid lips
Foretold the doom
Of these fair ships.

Ye waves that meet
Where strong tides surge
Again repeat
Grief's wail, and beat
King Hacon's dirge.

Far inland
Through labyrinthine clefts
Drifts
The invisible music —

Melodies melancholy-sweet
That rise and fall
In mournful cadences,
Until,
By secret rocky crevices
The green floods,
Winding through every part,
Their quest fulfil,
And beat with hollow thuds
Against the inmost wall
Of Orkney's island heart.

The hard sinews of the rocks
Relax;
Reef-ribbed skerries,
Wrack-robed,
Stretch their limbs;
And the old grey cliff,
Suddenly auriculate,
Leans seaward.
Cloud-veils,
Translucent in the morning light,
Hang from the shoulders of the hills,
And the fair face of the islands
Sparkles with pleasure.
Larks upleap to the sun,
And fling their wild sweet music on the air,
Flowers appear,
And where the bright heath springs
Linnet to linnet sings.

      'Tween cliff
      And hill

The vernal squill
Opens wide.
Stiff green leaves until,
Blue-eyed,
It stares in delight
At the bright
Colouring
Of the dress Spring wears,
And wonders why
Loveliness like this should be
On sea
And sky.

(*Coda*)

The strange peace of the north
Falls upon the waters;
Dim blue islands,
Sun-steeped in summer haze,
Transmuted into cloud
Glimmer,
And vanish...
The sea-vapours forget their birth,
And lie like lost Edens in the midst of the deep,
Half-asleep,
Lulled by the leisurely degrees
Of the sun's advance,
While in the compass of those beams that gird
Heaven's wide expanse
Not one faint sound is heard —
Only the slow turning of the earth,
The quiet breathing of the slumbering seas.

Italian Funeral

It was beside a farm
High in the Apennines
Among the green-leaved vines
And olives. Summer charm
And delight was in that yard:
Also a coffined pall
Set on two chairs, it being
A country funeral...

The ground was burnt and hard.
Barefoot peasants stood
Rooted to the spot
In patient attitude.
I, too, stood with them, seeing
An aged mother brought
By weeping women there,
To bid her son farewell.

They placed her in a chair.
Then, with bowed form and head,
Dumbly grouped in grief,
Waited before the dead.

(Of this I now would tell)

"Hand gropes for hand: this holds
An arm, and for relief
Another lightly lies
Upon a shoulder. Folds
Of head-cloth, like a shawl,
In long black rimples fall
Around their forms...

Anon,
Comforting words of prayer,
Full of sad benison,
Rise in the calm bright air. "

Watching with silent eyes
These women, thickly draped
In mourning garb, I saw
(Like thing that had escaped
My notice by some flaw)
It was, without a doubt,
A certain scene depicted
In old Italian art —
Veiled women grouped about
A mother sore afflicted...

He must have noticed, too,
Such mourning and such loss
Before his pencil drew,
Faithful to eye and heart,
His women at the Cross.

Italian Funeral [2]

Was it Fra Angelico, or some other
That painted once a certain "Crucifixion"
With women grouped around the virgin Mother?

Again I see the mournful valediction
Of that sad group like statue from the moulding —
Look, 'tis them indeed – without one contradiction —

Sculptured in grief, each to the other holding
Hand on shoulder as they linger thus a-weeping,
Rimpled head-cloths each bowed form enfolding.

So still, so motionless and yet unsleeping —
An artist saw them and the scene depicted
Beside the cross a patient vigil keeping.

Peasants they were, like those, by grief constricted,
Yet sought in silence their own grief to smother,
Comforting thus a parent sore afflicted.

[**Blind when a Boy**]

Blind when a boy, yet seeing cliff and wave
I knew not that my spirit was being bound
By invisible threads, of sight and sound and air
To chain my spirit to this alien land.
Among the rocks in pools of ware
The sun with threads of shining silk wove round
My innocent heart and the strong winds
Laid bonds upon me and I knew it not.
Ocean breathed subtle spells of potent smell...

Watch the young seals play in the breaking wave
Swimming along the shallow tide mark
Or follow me as I walk along the shore.
The storms of summer with its tourist crowds
Break the enchantment, but when winter comes
With gentle calm of vast eternal peace
And the boundless ocean melts...

Spring 1947

Now at the Willows
     'Tis Spring o' the year,
Young buds are breaking,
     Mornings are clear;
Blackbirds are singing
     Of Winter's demise,
Light winds are shaking
     The tops of the trees;
Green leaves are springing,
     Flowers appear,
Children are swinging
     In maddest career
Now at the Willows —
     He is not here.

Departure

My friend! – ah, thou art gone!
    No more for thee
    Morning's delight may be;
The silver-mantled dawn
    Is not for thee.

The seasons run their course —
    But not for thee.
    Ah! Not for thee
Beats landward now the hoarse
    And hollow-sounding sea.

Not now for thee
    The pageantry of Spring:
    The silent ecstasy
Of swallows on the wing
    Means naught to thee.

The moorland winds that blow
    Are not for thee.
    Not now for thee
Blossoms the wayside rose
    Or blooms the lilac tree!

A shadow, thou art gone,
    And canst not see
    What lovely things there be:
Earth puts her beauty on —
    But not for thee.

Zero

Lost in that land
Were west and east,
Of bird and beast
There was no sign.
The stationary sun
Vermilion red
Stood overhead.
On every hand
Gone come and past,
No rule or line
No first or last.
Deep down, in clay
Or rock not one
Fossil of fish or bone
With scale and claw
Frozen in stone.
There was no law
Of things to come,
No night or day,
Circle or square
To make one mark
On time or space,
Measure and trace
By angle or arc.

But something there
Not deaf nor dumb
Nor blind, that lay
Beyond the ken
Of mortal men.

In Memory of Sir William Wallace

A nation's thanks we owe thee, warrior chief,
    Whose knightly sword unsheathed in noble cause
    Redeemed from wrong fair Scotia's ancient laws,
Smote England's chains, and gave our land relief.

'God arms the patriot,' this thy firm belief
    Since sworn to heaven thy life allegiance was
    Nor could that high crusade of freedom pause
Till valour, conquering, succoured Scotland's grief.

Where beats with honest warmth the breast of
                                Scotland's chief
    In peer or peasant, ever as of yore,
    Once thou art named, brave Wallace, beatest more.

O Caledonia! Never be forgot
    This mountain spirit and the deathless love
Which, rising cloudlike, round his brow is caught.

Ode of Welcome to
Her Majesty Queen Elizabeth

on the Occasion of Her First Visit to Orkney

Kindle the flaming beacon on the Ward!
Look, watchman! 'Tis the ship! It comes our way!
Your patient vigil has its high reward.
Signal her swift approach – for lo, today,
    Past each historic spot
    Where Vikings ruled and fought
Speeds now through Scapa Flow with pennants gay
    Britannia's royal yacht.

As on review, the islands like a fleet
Float on the waves, awaiting her commands.
Flags stream aloft, and Orkney voices greet
The passing ship where she, our Monarch, stands.
    Prince Philip at her side
    Hail, too, with loyal pride!
Lift, silver waves, your crests, and clap your hands
    In homage far and wide.

Islands, make way, and for your noble Queen
Leave clear a sea-path in your clustered ranks.
Acclaim her, let your loyalty be seen:
Stand guard along your links and grassy banks.
    The bow-wave, as it breaks,
    Soft bright sea-music makes,
And isle to isle joins voice to give her thanks
    Who Rognvald's swan-road takes.

Join with us, seagulls on the wing
Who fly in freedom, scorning to be slaves.
Up, up, ye island larks, arise and sing,
And match your music with the singing waves.
    Farms, deck yourselves in green,
    On fields let flowers be seen.
Beat on your hollow drums, ye cliffs and caves,
    And cry, "The Queen, the Queen!"

Hither again comes one of royal race
To where Saint Magnus' shrine stands sentinel,
And we, within its walls, her lineage trace
From famous chiefs of whom our sagas tell.
    With deferential mien
    County and town convene,
While gaily now each loud cathedral bell
    Peals welcome to our Queen.

And we bid you, gracious Queen, farewell,
From every Orkney heart the words are said,
"Come quickly back! – that to our chronicle
Of ancient valour by the noble dead
    We, too, by counsels sage,
    May add another page,
And your bright fame in scaldic measures spread
    Through this your heritage."

Born 1854 [extract]

This old disseminator of parochial lore
Has reached his five score…
The redoubtable Gerald…
Returns to his office, and, putting on his specs
Puzzles himself over a dialect narrative by Lex,
Nods his head, and murmurs "This clean beats the Lallans
We'll put it in to give the adverts balance…
And if anyone should see a
Rare bird (the first in Scotland!) say, an *Ibex falcenellus*
(Someone is sure to write to the paper and tell us!)
Or the eighty whales captured at Rothiesholm
Or the twenty speckled porpoises at Scapa,
Or locusts in the north,
Or golden eagles seizing ducks at Rendall,
Write The Orcadian!
And with all this news of a hundred folk or more
At the Sands of Ness, taking spoots (sold in the
     Kirkwall streets at twopence a score!)…
And all the while the little tittle-tattle
Of local news and parish prattle
Keep them as happy as a bairn with a rattle.

But tak a care o' me,
I must stop, for here comes Geremy".

The Farmer

From the Swiss of Salomon Steinberg

He stands upon the road: carved out in black
    On evening clouds, behind him glowing red.
    And seems like one (so gravely set his head)
Who much had walked in sorrow's flinty track.

He casts upon my hands a strong keen glance:
    Those hold a bunch of fresh anemones.
    To me it seems as though he laughing says,
"Child, had *my* daily task so fair a chance!"

He then looks up: and in his eyes are seen
    A lake, brown honest acres that have borne
    Twice twenty thousand ears of waving corn,
Meadows with clover pastures, woodlands green.

He nods to me, and strides off in farewell
    Along the path toward his little field,
    And from his steps harsh sounds, as though they pealed
From driving plough-shares, o'er the mountain swell.

A Butterfly

From the Swiss of Richard B. Matzig

Dusky-velvet-golden butterfly,
Hoverst o'er my path in woodland light,
Dancing guidest thou my footsteps aright,
Sunbedrunken thing, tossed low and high.

All alone are we, thou sportest, I stride,
Fir-trees shadow like deepest night our way,
Dusky-velvet-golden dancer, stay,
Stay thus poised – a dream – along my side.

Copyrights Belonging to W. Wordsworth!

Celestial light.
Something that is gone.
The visionary gleam.
God, who is our home.
Heaven lies about us in our infancy.
The light and *whence* it flows.
The vision splendid.
That important Palace whence he came.
The eternal mind.
What was so fugitive.
Obstinate questionings of sense.
Words not realised.
High instincts.
Shadowy recollections.
The fountain light.
The eternal silence.
That immortal sea which brought us thither.

O Gatherer of glorious while
I leave to thee thy diction versatile,
And meekly now my spirit reconcile
To pedantry and labour mercantile.

The Farewell Sting

Ye insects d'Italia —
Depart! and farewell!
Your stings hypodermic
Gave many a sharp prick,
And made me to leap quick
With agonised yell!
O Parmesian Wasp,
That caused me to gasp,
You fastened your choice on
My innocent wrist,
Injecting your poison
Or ever I wist.
Go hence, or I'll strike you
And send you pell-mell,
For I do not like...

                    ...you,
Depart and farewell,
You swarms of mosquito,
Who worked in the dark
You made me your 'Vitto'
And left a sore mark...

O insects d'Italia,
You love me too well,
Ye insects d'Italia,
Depart and farewell!

Hogmanay 1928

Lightly lapped the minutes – Crack!
      "Ah," said the old year, "there goes
      Thorax, carapace, pincers, toes.
Shrimps! if I've not lost, alack,
My horny-skeletoned old back.
      And what to do awanting clothes,
      Is more than my poor body knows.
Ah, crack! confound the almanac!

"If only time and space were static,
      O what a comfort life would be,
      But I must shed (O pity me!)
My crusted creeds and vows dogmatic,
      To stiffen into certainty
The new *zeitgeist* of things aquatic."

Poet Myopicus

Reading with due decorum
"De Rerum Rusticorum",
He didna look afore him
    And trampt the bonnie floo'er
Scanning life's far horizon.
Him Chance took many a rise on
Who rarely had his eyes on
    The business o' the 'oor.

With eyeballs telescopic,
And vision half myopic,
He missed each nearer topic
    That bumped against his boot.
He'd watch a flying scorrie
Or distant Tammy-norrie
And walk right in a quarry
    With absent-minded foot.

His views of life and Nature
Disdained each narrow feature
In landscape or in creature —
    Except at fifty yards!
The bees that filled his bonnet
And hived in song or sonnet
Swarmed – take my word upon it —
    In skulls of ancient bards.

[Curly Kail]

Scorn not the Kailyard, Plastic, you have roared
Mindless of its green cabbage; tatties hot
Shakespeare enjoyed for dinner, in this plot
A small green shoot gave peas to Petrarch's board.
A thousand beans old Tasso here did hoard;
With it Camões flanked an exile's beef;
The Kailyard glittered with a fresh green leaf
Amid the mutton with which Dante stored
His vegetarian maw. A caterpillar vamp
Fair flegged mild Spenser, called from English glades
To struggle with cauld kail; and, when a damp
        Fell on MacDiarmid's mind, his garden spade
        Became loud sounding bagpipes whence he blew
Gael-animating strains, alas poor Hugh.

Limericks

There once was a missionary bishop
Who wanted some "dundies" to dish up.
        He wielded his wand
        With a wonderful hand,
And walloped some ten score of fish up.

Came to Orkney a man who was frantic
To angle upon the Atlantic.
        He soon was afloat
        In Willie's wee boat,
And caught some fishes gigantic.

His wife's good judgment allows 'er
To remonstrate, and say to him, "Now, Sir,
      You'll get a bad cold
      Just do what you're told —
And mind that nice crease in your trouser."

A lad from the land of the leal
Was nipped by a powerful partan
      He let go the creel
      With a horrible squeal
Saying "Let be for let be," that's sartan.

There was a pair in Venetzia
Celebrated a fine sposalitzia
      Said the man from the Pole
      In a fright, "Bless my soul!
I'm off – for this fairly beats ye!"

The folk in the train had a "vista"
Of a strange-looking Orkney "artista"
      With loud exclamation
      They saw his carnation
And cried "He's a wild Communista."

(I was wearing a red carnation in the train)

Hogmanay

Say not the warehouse doors are fettered
The managers and staff all gone,
Communications now are bettered
We simply use the Ansaphone.

If goods were cheap, drapers were buyers,
It may be in your shelves concealed
Forgotten stocks could wake desires
And Rendall's future orders yield.

For while the tired wives, vainly trying,
Fresh New Year bargains seek to gain,
Down south, through Arthur's clever buying
We may still higher sales attain.

And not alone our urgent letters
Send we when 6 o'clock strikes loud
But greetings from your grateful debtors
To all – including John MacLeod.

Coupon-Free

Say not your shopping naught availeth,
        The coupons and the chits are vain,
The Board of Trade faints not nor faileth,
        And, as in wartime, rules remain.

If goods are scarce, curtail desires;
        It may be, in the Corner Store,
Old Santa aids e'en now the buyers
        Who, but for you, have blocked the door.

For while the tired wives, Christmas-shopping,
        Can scarcely find a thing in stock,
Downstreet, at Rendall's Warehouse stopping,
        Troop in the Orkney country folk.

And not alone at Kirkwall windows,
        When Yuletide comes, the people stare:
Ideas for gifts come slow, how slowly,
        But Brigwards look – the goods are there!

Yule-tide at the Bridge

Christmas-tide in Kirkwall,
That old Cathedral city,
    The Yule-tide ba', with its tramp o' feet,
    Pushes its way through the narrow street;
    A wilder scrimmage you'll never meet;
But, to begin my ditty,
    To see the townsfolk fairly beat
'Bout presents was a pity.

Gifts!
They teased the ladies till wits were scattered,
    And close-bobbed heads with thought were
        cracking,
While nothing but choice of presents mattered
    To the goodmen all as vainly racking
Their wearied brains with what to send
To niece and cousin, uncle, friend;
    Each cries, "Come, tell me what to do.
What else, wife, would you recommend?"
    While sisters and brothers
    Fathers and mothers
Stared at the ceiling till all looked blue.

At last the people, faint and nervous,
    To the Corner warehouse wended:
"'Tis clear," cried they, "the Bridge will serve us —
    And as for Rendall's – why, 'tis splendid
To see those large front windows shining.
With the very nick-nacks for which we're pining —
Suede fur-topped gloves with woolly lining.
    We hope, just here, with right good reason,
    To solve the problem of the season.

Rouse up, sirs! Empty all those cases
Of trinkets, fal-de-rals and laces,
Or else we'll put you through your paces!
 At this the draper and each apprentice
 Sprang round like athletes in their twenties.
A week of Christmas trading!
 Out spake the haberdasher:
"'Tis time, I think, for barricading.
 These good-folks all grow rasher —
D'ye think it's easy to hand you down
Choice gifts for only half-a-crown;
The shop's nigh emptied by the town —
 O for a seat, a seat, a seat!"
Just as he said this, what should beat

On the topmost stair but a tramp of feet.
 "Bless us," cried the draper, "what's that?
If more are coming I'm done – that's flat!
Can another bargain-hunting batch
Be climbing in through the open hatch?
 This Xmas trade! If it grows much faster,
 Sold out we'll be – a queer disaster,
Only an echoing in the lum?
It sounds like customers' footsteps come.
Much more, then – pandemonium!"

"Come down," the mercer said with vigour.
Down stairs there came, a Yule-tide figure,
 Whose ruddy countenance and merry
 Shone brightly as a polished berry;
His long red coat was edged with white,
And he himself was plump and tight;
The children shouted with delight
 Quoth one, "In spite of storm and rain,

He, hearing of Kirkwall's dreadful plight
(He got it by wireless last night),
   Has come this way in his aeroplane."

He advanced to the front shop section;
"Kirkwall," quoth he, by my direction
   May purchase gifts from out this sack
   Whatever the lovely ladies lack —
   'Tis the twenty-fourth by the almanack —
Perfumes, bangles, purses, dresses
   Have pity, I pray you, on my poor back,
Which a heavy load oppresses.
   Then up to the crowd old Santa stept
With merriest laughter shaking:
   "Good folks," said he, "I am yclept
   A ready giver, but a great adept
I also am at taking."
"Yes," laughed he, "twelve months ago
   I relieved of a mint o' money
Some kindly dames and Oh! – heigh ho!
I fairly made the siller flow
   Till everyone was stony.
And I can rid your town from grasp
   Of florin – tanner – sovereign."
   "Can you?" was the astonished gasp
   Of the crowd around him hovering.
Then were his hands for parcels fumbling.
Till you heard a rustling and a rumbling,
Like as it were an avalanche crumbling;
And the crumbling grew to a mumbling,
And the mumbling grew to a mighty jumbling,
As out of the sack the things came tumbling.
   Necklets, Hankies, Scarfs and Dresses,

Shirts and Sweaters, Ties, Tie-presses,
Braces – otherwise called straps —
Men's Pyjamas, Collars, Caps,
Shetland Shawls, and Shoulder Haps;
Overcoats in tweeds and naps,
    Cardigans and Tunic Belts;
    Mens' Soft Hats – Velours and Felts —
Ladies' Jumpers, Furs and Frocks;
Babies' Dresses; Hoods and Socks,
    Tea Cloths, Tray Cloths, Rugs and Mats,
    Cushion Covers, Stockings, Hats;
Perfumes, Fancy Soaps and Beads,
Dolls and Rattles, Wooden Steeds —
    And men and women, with loud applause,
    Greeted the salesman – Santa Claus.

And I must not omit to mention
    That in Kirkwall town there's a people,
Whose dress attracts as much attention
    As the Auld Kirk's pointed steeple,
For their stylish, smart, distinctive dresses,
Make stranger-bodies take deep guesses
Whence these handsome-garbed princesses.
"What shop," cried they, "could so adorn her?"
    As a well-dressed lady passes,
"What shop but RENDALL'S at the Corner!"
    Laughed back the Kirkwall lasses.

"So, folks," said Santa, "all is well
    If you'll heed my last advising
Be one of RENDALL'S clientelle,
    Results will be surprising,
For, though they fleece you to your last brown copper,
You'll get some rattling bargains as is proper."

The Armada of 1588

What were the ships the Pope did bless?
What victory the Huns did miss?
What wreckage strewed our shores like this? —
    The Hunnish Spanish 'Mada.

With gallant sail they left their port;
The boisterous winds they were its sport;
Of victory they did come short —
    Invincible Armada.

On fiendish work they sailed apace,
To sink our ships from ocean's face;
But dauntless Britons left no trace
    Of German-Spanish 'Mada.

The ships were wrecked, the sailors drowned;
Those saved were by the natives found;
They fell in love with girls around —
    The bonnie northern lasses.

The girls were taught to knit the hap
And lovely shawls and Fair Isle cap
Their pretty girls in which to wrap —
    Thus did the sailor laddies.

The relics of those Spanish tools,
The dupes of wicked German fools,
Is handed down in shawls and "cools".
    As seen in RENDALL'S warehouse.

Now you should be a patriot true
And buy a shawl of Shetland 'oo,
And socks of gold, red, white, and blue
    As shown in RENDALL'S window.

The Battle of Kirkwall Bridge

The Battle of Kirkwall Bridge
In Spring nineteen-fifteen
Bids fair to be the greatest
That the town has ever seen.
The SLAUGHTER will be awful and
The FIRING most intense.
The INVADERS' AMMUNITION
Will be silver, gold and pence.
The first FORT to be taken
Is the furnishing depot
Where the floorcloth and linoleum
And rugs must be laid low.
There's mats and curtains, window poles
And what-nots, tables, chairs.
There's carpets suited for each corner
And carpets for the stairs.
To help to make a GRAND ASSAULT
Upon the common FOE
Assistance has been given
By the firm GR and Co.
There will be TACKLED oilskins,
Coats and trousers, skirts and frocks,
Caps, gloves and collars, mufflers, ties
And shirts and hose and socks;
GR is now so well PREPARED
For this part of the FIGHT.
The LEADERS have decided
That the CHARGES will be light
In suitings, blousings, trouserings
And flannelette so fine.
The SPOIL for the BESIEGERS

Will provide a small goldmine.
The INNER FORTRESS strongly held
By millinery styles
Is sure to fall by STRATEGY
To Kirkwall ladies' smiles
And when the FIGHT is ended and
When PEACE has been proclaimed
The timid ones who TOOK NO PART
Are sure to be ashamed.
The old firm calls for MORE RECRUITS,
The fight is raging so
Haste! Buckle on your silver sword
And join GR and Co.

Rendall's Bazaar

Jeemie has been to the town, and has just come out of
the bus with a big parcel. He enters the social centre of
the parish where a dozen or so farmers and their wives
are discussing local topics.

JEEMIE – Friends, Yamils, Orkneymen – Look for
     your cash!
   I'm back with goods from Rendall's, let me praise
     them.
   The money which we spend returns again;
   What's saved lies idle in the stocking-foot:
   So be it spent at Rendall's. Whiskered Santa
   Has told you Rendall's is the Xmas Warehouse;
   If he has not, I'll advertise it now,
   And royally will Rendall's answer it.
   Here, under leave of Santa, and our friends —

For Santa is a shrewd old gentleman,
And Rendall's, too, an old-established firm —
Come I to speak of Rendall's gay bazaar.
Friends, What a shop! – Cramful of Xmas gifts;
For Santa's made his KIRKWALL Depôt there —
And Santa is a shrewd old gentleman.
O you should see the Leather Handbags, Purses,
Tall Perfume-sprays, Puff-bowls, and "Yardley" Sets,
Boxes of Ladies' "Lissue" Hankies, Satchets,
Brush Cases, Combs, Work-baskets, Stocking-hoops,
Small Needle-cases, Combs, and Knitting Bags,
Fur-lined Suede Gloves, Tea-aprons, Knitted Jumpers,
Cushions and Runners, Coloured Table Cloths,
Tie-sets, Tie-presses, Shirts, Pyjamas, Socks,
Sweaters and Scarfs – but see them for yourselves:
I speak but to confirm what Santa said,
You all believed him "once" – NOT WITHOUT
    CAUSE!
What cause withhold you, then, to ACT for him.
O Christmas, thou art fled the chimney-top,
And men are losing bargains. Bear with me,
My cash is in the register at Rendall's,
But you shall see how it comes back to me (opens
    his parcel).

1ST FARMER – Methinks there is some profit in his
    sayings.

2ND FARMER – If thou consider rightly of the matter,
    Rendall's have rattling bargains.

3RD FARMER –   Have they not, Tammie?
    I fear we can send farther, and buy worse.

4TH FARMER – Marked ye his words, "Old Santa's
  Kirkwall Depôt"?
  Therefore, 'tis certain it's the Christmas Warehouse.

JEEMIE – This Christmastide the Corner Warehouse
  might
  Supply the county's needs. 'Tis crammed with stuff,
  And none so poor but they can purchase there.
  O Farmers, if I were disposed to stir
  Your fingers after pocket-book or purse,
  I should save Orkney pounds and Kirkwall pounds:
  See, here's an invoice with the name of Rendall's:
  I got it with my goods. 'Tis signed and paid.
  Let but the good-wives see the keen low prices —
  Which, pardon me, I do not mean to give —
  They'd helter-skelter to the Corner Shop
  And rush the counters with their last half-crown.
  Yea, buy quaint trinkets, priced one shilling each,
  And, as slight tokens of a green good-will,
  Distribute them in light Yule-hearted glee
  Among their neighbours.
4TH FARMER – Out with it, then. Read us the
  Invoice.
ALL – The prices, the prices. We will hear Rendall's
  prices.
JEEMIE – Have patience, gentle friends, I must not
  read them.
  It is not wise to tell how Rendall's serve you.
  You are not dukes, nor millionaires, but folk
  Who love to save, and hearing Rendall's price,
  It will persuade you, it will make you buy.
  'Tis good you should not know how cheap they are;
  For, if you should, you'd spend your last bawbee.

4TH FARMER – Out with the prices! Hurrah! Rendall's
    Invoice!

JEEMIE (displaying his purchase) – If you have cash,
    prepare to spend it now.

  You all do see this dress – 'Twas one pound five.

  Look, here's Gents' Ties at one and six apiece.

  See what a Shirt is yours for eight and six,

  And two nice Collars matching with the stuff.

  Judge, O ye farmers, how George Rendall's serve you!

  O, now you run; and, I perceive, you feel

  How deep your pockets are. The money clinks!

  Good friends, good friends, let me not stir you up

  To such a sudden flood of purchasing

ALL – We're off to Rendall's!

1ST FARMER – We'll seek the Corner Warehouse.

2ND FARMER – Away then. Out with the bus.

3RD FARMER – Hurrah! Christmas for ever!

4TH FARMER – Round the Mainland – this is
    Orkney's chance.

JEEMIE – O now they run, bus, bicycle and gig,
  For Orkney's highways meet at Olaf's Brig.

Brig News

To Rendalls! ye people from East and from West;
Through all the wide county, their gear is the best.
For Carpets and Hearthrugs they equals have none,
And Inlaid Linoleums that never wear done
Till an ordinary life-time is over. And oh! —
Was ever a Warehouse like G. R. & Co.'s?

They've Leather Suit Cases and strong Cabin Trunks
For emigrants travelling – soon sick in their bunks —
Stumpy Umbrellas, whose covers of silk
Keep all that's beneath them as snug as a whelk.
O, people keep running to Rendalls just like
An auld knowin' horse tae an auld feelie dyke.

They stayed not for brake, and stopped not for bus
They scurried tae Kirkwall with unco great fuss,
And e'er they arrived at the turn o' the Brig,
They scarcely left room for so much as a gig,
For a rare place for bargains and Ladies' Spring Shows
Is the Big Corner Warehouse, George Rendall & Co.'s.

A dame looked at Cretonne, a lad took it down.
"Here's Curtain Material – the finest in town.
Good wide Shadow Tissue, reversible too.
And dainty Lace Blinding: these patterns are new.
For Casements, Long Curtains, just take a bit turn
Awa' doon tae Rendall's, nearly at the Burn."

One look in the purse, one word to the lad,
Twelve yards of new Sun-proof Material she had.
The joy of a purchase quite loosened her cash
Long guarded so well; the matron grew rash,

And called for the draper to spread forth more wares —
Brush Doormats and Rugs for the feet o' the stairs.

There was lowsing o' bundles o' Covers and Sheets
And handling o' Easy Chairs padded in seats.
There was rugsing at Mattresses, lifting o' Beds,
Till the sweating assistants nigh lost all their heads.
Near the Window Poles swinging, with fittings all gilt,
Was spread many a Blanket and Eider Down Quilt.

To Rendall's, ye farmers from parish and isles,
For Heavy Tweed Suits in the latest o' styles;
Tight Oilskins, thick Guernseys, strong Wincey Shirts too,
Pullovers and Cardigans – there's one to fit YOU.
O' all wir good drapers, wherever you go,
You never find better than G. R. & Co.

Art and Appetite

*If the public could not swallow art without morning coffee or afternoon
tea, then both must be provided.*

— *Mr Stanley Cursiter, Director of the National Gallery of Scotland.*

The common folk may then applaud
High art, and enter in unawed.
      Why, even Philistines may risk it!
And in some decorated room
With abstract air of ease consume
      Picasso with a chocolate biscuit,
While waiters glide with café noir
      And recommend the Blake,
Or nod to patrons at the bar,
      "Yes, sir! Just half a shake!"
        "Some tea, sir?"
        "Paul Klee, sir?"
"A trifle of Cézanne?"
      "You'd like, sir,
        Van Dyck, sir,
Served up with marzipan."

Fragments

Si Deus Nobiscum

In sagas of Orkney we're told
Of battles on the sea
Fought by the Vikings brave and bold
. . . .

. . . .
. . . .
. . . .
. . . .

The Bishop in the palace hall
Had shield and coat of arms
And fighting men within his call
To guard 'gainst war's alarms.

The Viking cry to quake did cause
And sealed their foeman's doom
Yet over all the motto was
Si Deus nobiscum

Though now the Viking path is o'er,
Each bishop in his tomb,
Retains the device as before
Si Deus nobiscum

Upon the walls of Kirkwall School
This motto is inscribed

Teaching the lesson beautiful
From whom our help's derived.

And as the bishops represent
The scholars of their day
So now the Kirkwall school presents
The learned of Orcady.

Thus young Orcadians, side by side
In every desk and room
Look on these ancient words with pride
Si Deus nobiscum

    This is my nom-de-plume
Si Deus nobiscum

[Life's Supremest Good is Won]

Know, then, that life's supremest good is won
From inward harmony; and lies for man
Not less in leisured wisdom than
In strong deeds dared and done.

[The Islands]

I've seen them from a plane
Lie like green fragments of broken delft
Thrown down and scattered on a wide bare floor
And from a high vantage looked across
The sundering sounds tracing their separate
                              outline – bay and point —
Or the contours of distant island hills.

Epithalamium [extract]

The ancient Romans sang in Latin
Of ladies dressed in silk and satin,
Of gentle Lesbia and her sparrow
And Cupid with his bow and arrow
Poets each praised his damsel fair —
Her eyes, her nose, her feet, her hair,
And in good flowing rhyme and metre
Called her his own dear Margarita,
For in the proper Latin tongue
This meant a PEARL, such as was hung
From ladies' ears, or set in rings
To be the loveliest of things...

I, in my time, have gathered shells,
In which the margarita dwells,
But never a pearl found I – what's more
I'm still a carefree bachelor.

She'll be an ornament and grace
Whenever James may show his face.
She'll fill his home with light and lustre
Even when using a broom and duster
She'll cook the soup and swing the ladle,
She'll sweep the floor and rock the cradle,
She'll be his treasure through the years,
Her voice like music in his ears.
She'll wear beneath a smiling face
A steadfast will and heart of grace.
We wish them both love's richest boon
(Two hearts that beat in time and tune),
Tonight they've plighted each their troth:
GOD KEEP THEM! Blessings on them both

A Farewell Address [extract]

What ploys of paint or words or wool or speech
Have filled our winter evenings, each and each
Have meddled with some homely art or craft
And always in at something nice and daft.

Bessie will still supremacy maintain
With fluent brush, and Chrissie with the pen,
Ernest has gone, but Embla still remains
Our modest critic with the Mooney bairns.

An Old English Manor

What's this? Wir Scottish kith an' kin!
Douce Lowland burghers thick an' thin
An' sic a lack o' discipline
        Wi' tavern mugs
Auld Reekie's gleesome sangs an' din
Another wind as rugs
Auld Reekie's too'ers
Auld Reekie's motley din
Fair deaves me jugs
Wi' Scottish kith an' kin!
What!

Sent

O hearken to Israel's choir
 Chanting a psalm divine
As the music rises higher
From cymbal, trumpet, lyre
 In the courts of the sacred shrine
The chorus outpasses the gate
 Wreathed over with golden vine
The temple-stones, early and late
 Shout Glory, O Lord is Thine
And the multitude cry "Amen"
For Jehovah outpoureth anew
 A blessing on Palestine

Awake O ye tribes, awake
 Sing praises to God Most High
By whose word were the heavens made
And the worlds from pillars laid
 In the depth of the open sky.
On hilltop, valley and field
 The emblems of Paradise lie
 Creation a . . . . is sealed
 Unread by irreverent eye
And this hallowed house of God
Rings with symbol which none . . . .
 A mute mysterious cry.

As clouds in the sunny height
   Fling shadows along the land
As stars in the vault of night
On the lake reflect their light
   To the margin of the strand,
So in Zion's mountain see
   The city celestial stand.
A holier Sanctuary see
   Undefiled by tool or hand
Far from archetype unbuilt
By the craft of human guild
   Where Salem's pillars planned.

[Through Thicket, Bracken and Thorn]

Into the heart of the haunted wood
I pressed my way, through thicket, bracken
And thorn: there was no retreat.
The wild briar caught my feet.

[If We Our Minds Used to Discern]

If we our minds used to discern
The lessons which we all could learn
From things that we surround
We'd oft'ner search the shore

Textual Variants

A Country Burial [extra]

The world-old sorrow
(Wiser than our joy),
That first filled my heart
In the plank-seated barn
Left me; and looking
On the fast-filling grave
And then upon the earth
With its farms and its fields,
I smiled at what I knew
Of the soul that escaped
E'er the grave-digger came
With his old red spade.

The Night Wind

The moon slid under a cloud —
    She had seen a white ship sailing,
    A pitiless wind, and a mariner's wailing
Hushed in a watery shroud.

But to me it sang of a ship
    On far-off voyages riding,
    Till I heard the splash of the wave's dividing
And the rising bowline's drip,

The delicate fall of the foam
    The lapping of wider waters
    The laughter of sea-loving, sea-faring, yachters
Afloat on their fathomless home.

I listened all night to the sound
    Of sea-ditties, deeply throated —
    'Twas a mariners' chorus: faintly it floated
From a vessel homeward bound.

Departure [fourth stanza]

    No, not for thee
Night's treasures are displayed,
    Nor now for thee
    Sparkles her jewelry,
Like gems on violet laid.

Death

A moorland cottage, left of yore
    Untenanted and lone,
With crazy windows cobwebbed o'er
    And walls of crumbling stone.

Weep they for this, who ventured far
    Across the ocean foam?
What if, beneath some southern star
    They found a happier home?

I peered in through the windows twain
    Of an old house of clay.
But ah! – the living soul had ta'en
    A voyage worlds away.

The walls were wasted, and they fell
    On the wind-swept moors of death.
But whither walk, if ye can tell,
    The spirit and the breath?

Stromness [2] [first and fourth stanzas]

Stromness – a town whose narrow streets remain
An artist's delight whose huddle of houses and lanes
Composes a picture of cubes triangles and planes

Stromness – a town which its ancient beauty retains
An artist's delight with its huddle of lanes
Composing a picture of cubes, triangles and planes

Hoy's saurian loops, by time and tempest scarred,
With sinuous strength uprear on silent guard
And o'er the little town keep watch and ward.

Hoy's saurian hills uprear on silent guard
Their sinuous loops, by time and tempest scarred,
And on the little town keep watch and ward.

Hoy, with its sinuous ridges weathered and scarred,
Up from the ocean emerges like saurian guard,
And over the slumbering town keep innocent ward.

Sunset [3]

Mourn not the sunless sun:
See how the radiant clouds
Gather when day is done.

Ebb Tide

Now from the pool the swirling tide recedes,
    And from its waveless surface filtered falls
Peace, down to deeps where flaunt the green sea-weeds,
    Fanning their fronds, fearless of ocean squalls.
Slow patient limpets scythe the meads aquatic,
    And rosy crinoids radiate starry twinkles;
Hermits again with scuttlings acrobatic
    Dispute old claims on vacant periwinkles.
Anemones expand their hungry tentacles,
And earnest buckies keep their social conventicles.

A Cliff Conversation

Look! Down there below
Where the water is dark
Glides with menacing motion
A huge basking shark.
Young fulmars make merry
And swing to and fro
Out on the ocean
Dive scarfies for fish
On the edge of the skerry
Foam lies like white lace
And oh, I could wish —
    "Boy, come back from the face."

Rule Thou in Majesty Divine

Wisdom, strength, and praise unending
Be Thine, O God, all worlds transcending
   In Thy high glory's holiest height.
Mighty angels bow before Thee:
The hosts of Thy redeemed adore Thee,
   Who dwellest in eternal light.
   By Thy right arm alone
   Death's kingdom is o'erthrown.
     Hallelujah!
   Forth from the dead
   By Him, our Head,
   Captivity is captive led.,

Worship, thanks, and adoration
Be Thine, since Thou for our salvation
   Hast love's divinest purpose crowned.
Praise to Him who by Thy pleasure
Is made of Thy rich grace the measure,
   E'en Him in Whom our peace is found.
   Before Thy throne we fall,
   O Thou who fillest all.
     Hallelujah!
   Now Thine are we,
   Alone to Thee
   We lift our song exultantly.

Honour, riches, power, and blessing
Be Thine, O Lord, all things possessing.
    Be glory and dominion Thine!
Thou, in whom all fullness dwelleth,
Whose handiwork Creation telleth,
    Rule Thou in majesty divine.
       We laud Thee, and adore,
       God blessed for evermore.
         Hallelujah!
       Thy Name be sung
       By every tongue,
       To Thee the golden harps be strung.

On An Engraving [second stanza]

In calf-bound volume have I read his deep,
    His weighty discourse, preached in godly fear,
And well have marked how he in mind did keep
    The under-shepherd's motto graven here:
"Sermons take not from men's applause renown,
The people's practice is the preacher's crown."

Notes on the Poems

We provide the date and source of each text – when known – pointing out some significant details. While we have printed the poet's glosses as found in books and newspapers, in the notes that follow, we have added a few of our own where such seemed necessary, as we feel that a number of other words and allusions might seem impenetrable and difficult to research, to readers lacking access to relevant works of reference.

The great majority of poems have been taken from two sources. First, the four published books and second, manuscripts, typescripts, fair copies and press cuttings in the Orkney Library's Archives, Kirkwall: D 27/1–8, with a letter from Rendall to James Fergusson (23 April 1947, D 27/7/1) particularly useful for dating the earliest items.

COUNTRY SONNETS & Other Poems (1946), page 45.
Dedicated To My Mother

Foreword to the First Edition, by Hugh Marwick, O.B.E., D. Litt.

"Good wine needs no bush," and Mr Rendall's desire that I should write a few lines to introduce the following poems can be ascribed only to his own innate modesty. For the quality of his vintage is not in doubt, and any commendation of mine is merely redundant, if not presumptuous.

On the formal side, these poems in their metrical technique bear the stamp of the skilled craftsman, and one is often reminded of the author's familiarity with modern prosodic experiments – notably those of Bridges. On the other hand, the essential qualities of Mr. Rendall's poetry are not at all derivative, but intensely personal and characteristic. The poems here included are not poems of passion or of dramatic moments. Rather do they conform to the Wordsworthian theory of poetry as having its origin in 'emotion recollected in tranquillity.' In each poem can be seen the poetic response to some aspect of life or nature of a singularly sensitive imaginative mind, and the reader's appreciation will be in exact proportion to his own sensibility.

In tone and background these poems are again reminiscent of Wordsworth, whose interpretation of the Stock-dove's message is the happiest comment possible on Mr. Rendall's work.

> "He sang . . . .
> "Of serious faith, and inward glee."

So also, as in the case of the shepherd-lord,

> "Love had he found in huts where poor men lie,
> "His daily teachers had been woods and rills
> "The silence that is in the starry sky,
> "The sleep that is among the lonely hills."

And lastly – Mr Rendall would certainly declare with Wordsworth himself

> "'Tis my delight, alone in summer shade,
> "To pipe a simple song for thinking hearts."

Such is the content, such the temper of this present volume. The product of a highly cultured and fastidious mind, it adds distinction to the small but treasured garden of native Orcadian verse, and is in consequence assured of warmest welcome in Orkney itself. But true poetry transcends all boundaries, and it may be confidently predicted that this little book, by reason of its inherent grace and beauty, will be cherished wherever it is read by all who can hear the horns of elfland blow.

H. MARWICK.
Kirkwall.

Dedicatory Verses, page 46. 1946?

The Shepherds, page 47. 14 February 1943. Original title The Pastoral Poets.

Longing for a Country Life, page 48. 1941.

Winter Mood, page 49. 12 January 1943. Original title Rustic Toil.

Orkney Landscape, page 50. 1926–30.

Birsay, page 51. 1940–46.

Varro Dedicates His Book, page 52. 1940–46. Marcus Terentius Varro, 116–27BC, great scholar most of whose books are lost; began the farming guide for his wife Fundania in his eightieth year.

St Gregory of Nazianzus Bids Farewell to His Bishopric, page 53. 1943. St Gregory of Nazianzus, 330–390, also known as "Gregory the Theologian", Archbishop of Constantinople; holder of Nicene views who wrote prolifically on theology.

Wide Waters, page 54. 14 June 1926. Printed in *The Kirkwallian*, magazine of Rendall's school, No. 7, New Series, July 1926.

Siberian Spring, page 55. 1926–30. Cf *The House of the Dead*, Everyman's Library, 1911 translation. Early in Part II, "Summer Season", as Nature is awakening, *the convict in his chains feels the trembling influence of the lovely days...*

A Dedication, page 56. 1946?

David the Shepherd, page 57. 1917 or 1918.

St Athanasius, page 58. Printed in *The Orkney Herald*, 9 February 1927. St Athanasius, 293–373, Pope Athanasius I of Alexandria; strongly disputed Arian views.

The Praise of Beauty, page 60. 1928. Originally The Imperishable Thing, it was sent by Rendall to J. C. Squire of *The London Mercury*, who replied in February 1928: *It is not bad & we'd gladly consider more: but it hasn't the last degree of tightness.* That characteristic was what Rendall saw in The Greek Anthology which, he wrote, *in translation had a direct influence on me in my twenties in showing the virtues of "tightness".* Only stanza 1 of the original was printed in *Country Sonnets*. The first verse appears as The Imperishable Thing, page 235.

Beauty's Quest, page 61. 1917–18. Rendall wrote, *the original had 7 stanzas and had 'Bridges' written all over it!*

Summer Flowers, page 62. 1946? Rendall: *recent (also an experiment).*

The Wooing of the Rose, page 64. 30 April 1927.

Winter, page 65. 1918–26. Four stanzas were dropped from the typescript, described by Rendall as "early". They have been printed on page 258.

Flower Ghosts, page 66. 1918–26. Original title A Morning Dream, *an experiment introducing double stresses, and the kind of rhythms you have noticed but did not care for,* wrote Rendall to Fergusson.

The Night Wind, page 67. 1926. Four stanzas were omitted from *Country Sonnets*. They are reprinted on page 319.

Orkney, page 67. 1918–26?

In a Churchyard, page 68. 1918–26?

The Fisherman, page 68. 1918–26? Original title The Sailor's Grave, in *Scots Variations to the Greek Anthology.* The version in *Country Sonnets* was improved by the few changes in the other three versions surviving.

leid: lead (sinker)   *yamils*: contemporaries

Andrew Lang's translation of
LEONIDAS OF TARENTUM.

Theris the Old, the waves that harvested
More keen than birds that labour in the sea,
With spear and net, by shore and rocky bed,
Not with the well-manned galley laboured he;
Him not the star of storms, nor sudden sweep
Of wind with all his years hath smitten and bent,
But in his hut of reeds he fell asleep,
As fades a lamp when all the oil is spent:
This tomb nor wife nor children raised, but we
His fellow-toilers, fishers of the sea.

Orkney Crofter, page 69. c.1946? "Recent".

The Town, page 70. 22 January 1930.

From the German of Theodor Storm.

Die Stadt	The town
Am grauen Strand, am grauen Meer	By the gray shore, by the gray sea
Und seitab liegt die Stadt; —	And close by lies the town —
Der Nebel drückt die Dächer schwer,	The fog rests heavy round the roofs
Und durch die Stille braust das Meer	And through the silence roars the sea
Eintönig um die Stadt.	Monotonously round the town.

Es rauscht kein Wald, es schlägt im Mai   No forest murmurs, and no bird sings
Kein Vogel ohn' Unterlaß;   Unceasingly in May;
Die Wandergans mit hartem Schrei   The wand'ring goose with raucous cry
Nur fliegt in Herbstesnacht vorbei,   On autumn nights just passes by,
Am Strande weht das Gras.   On the shoreline waves the grass.

Doch hängt mein ganzes Herz an dir,   Yet all my heart remains with you,
Du graue Stadt am Meer;   O gray town by the sea;
Der Jugend Zauber für und für   Youth's magic ever and a day
Ruht lächelnd doch auf dir, auf dir,   Rests smiling still on you, on you,
Du graue Stadt am Meer.   O gray town by the sea.

A Country Burial, page 71. 11 February 1927. The last twelve lines of the original were not printed in *Country Sonnets*. We print them in the Newly Collected section, p318.

Kirkyard by the Shore, page 71. 1946?

The Knowe, page 72. 1 July 1927. Original title, The Sailors' Knowe, in two stanzas. Lines 6–8 were changed to the version in *Country Sonnets*, from

> *When evening falleth, we can feel*
> *The patient homeward-wending tread*
> *Of fishers each with laden creel.*

On the handwritten original there is an attractive pen and ink sketch by Rendall of the scene described.

Cliff Grave, Hoy, page 73. 2 July 1927. Originally The Miners' Graves. Like "The Knowe", "preserved by local tradition".

Town-Dwellers, page 73. 11–12 August 1942. Original title Town Life.

Scarabrae Re-Visited, page 74. Printed in *The Orkney Herald*, 19 November 1928.

ORKNEY VARIANTS & Other Poems (1951), page 77

Dedicatory Verses to Miss Janet Couper, page 78. 1951?

> *the Place*: the village round the Earl's Palace, Birsay

To the Compositors and Printers of this Book, page 80. 24 November 1950.

> *lintick*: linnet

POEMS IN DIALECT, page 81

The dialect used in these poems is a thin survival from the speech of the ancient Norse earldom, diluted by Scots' idioms and vocabulary, and now heard only in a context of common English.

Cragsman's Widow, page 81. 9 December 1946. Original title Cliff Accident. Printed in *The Glasgow Herald*, 26 May 1947. Rendall speculated: *I wonder what he* [James Fergusson] *would say if he knew that Cliff Accident was inspired by the vagaries of the Plastic school?* (Letter to Ernest Marwick.)

Writing to Fergusson, Rendall stated: ... *used IMAGINA-TIVELY, the dictionary can be one of the most fascinating of books. (The mental 'pictures' of my "Cliff Accident" came out of the Orkney Norn, though their imaginative FRAME came from remembered conversations with old Westray fishermen and of their language.*

swappan the mallimaks: catching fulmars

By wi' the Sea, page 81. 25 June 1949, in *The Glasgow Herald*.
steethe: foundation   *whummle*: turn over

Salt i' the Bluid, page 82. 17 November 1950. Original title Salt in the Blood. The version in *Orkney Variants* has several changes, including omission of the second stanza.

The rafters rigg'd ebeun me heid
Are wissen'd and black wi' the sea:
Me widden box-bed was fashioned and meid
Fae planks of "The Merry Lea".

gouster: storm violently
whaal-backs: long smooth waves (lit. whale-backs).

The Planticru, page 83. 30 April 1948. In *The Orcadian*, 12 May 1949. A few changes in the second stanza improved dialect and rhythm. In *The Glasgow Herald*, 28 May 1949.

planticru: small kailyard; walled enclosure.

Mansie's Threshing, page 84.

Lady's Elwand: belt of Orion	*fleep*: loose fold
twart-backs: cross-beams	*barrow-wight*: creature from
minted: darkly hinted	burial mound
skroo: small stack	*mettins*: seeds of grain
Pickie-knowe: Pict-knoll	*spret*: sprang up
bockie: frightening creature	

Shore Tullye, page 87. Replying to a letter from Tom Scott, of 23 January 1965, Rendall expressed his pleasure in the inclusion of this poem in Scott's *Oxford Anthoogy of Scottish Verse*: *...because of its intricate metrical structure* [it] *was something of a tour de force.*

In his note in *Orkney Variants*, Rendall explained: *This is an attempt to render into Orkney dialect the court measure of the ancient scalds. The incident is traditional, and "the pirate's grave" can still be seen on the hill-side above Rackwick, Hoy.*

krugglan: crouching   *fleep*: useless fellow, sluggard
congles: large boulders

ORKNEY VARIANTS, page 88
These Variants are not strict verbal translations, but transpose into an Orkney setting poems whose foreign originals depict some universal aspect of life.

On Reading some Translations from the Greek Anthology, page 88. There's a recording of Rendall reading several poems, including this one, in the Orkney Library's Archive: Ernest W. Marwick, D 31/TR/75, c.1966.

Celestial Kinsmen, page 89. May 1947. In *The Glasgow Herald*, 28 May 1949, as one of "Three Orkney Variants". Three versions exist, quite different in several respects. The text in this book is best in form and language. On 2 May 1947, Rendall wrote: *Today I found a word that will confound them all: 'tulliment'...*

tullimentan: scintillating

Contentment, page 89. In *The Glasgow Herald* as one of "Three Orkney Variants', 28 May 1949.
bruck'd aboot: pottered or drudged about

Doun at the P'lace, page 90. On 6 May 1947, Rendall wrote to James Fergusson: *One difficulty we have in using our Orkney vocabulary is that we have true native words which have an exact equivalent in Scots but a different meaning e.g. blyde with us is used in the sense of 'to be fond of' – to be blyde of somebody, and is never used in the sense of 'happy'.* But see the last line on p161.

He glossed *blyde* as fond in this book. His last line seems to have better tone and associations than John Buchan's rendering of the same text (1917):

For Oh! I love common life!

lythe: pollack

Haad Aff, Haad Aff the Pleugh, page 90.

Envy, page 91. 1945–46?

madrum: frenzy, jealous rage

Plain Fare: Guid Lear, page 91.

glaip: gulp

The Happy Isle, page 91. In *The Glasgow Herald*, 28 May 1949.
muify: close, warm
ooran: lowing softly, making low, contented sounds
hallan: cross-beams on which the hens roost
gloondie: gluttonous
peerie: little

The Twa, page 92. 1948? Writing on 15 December 1948, James Fergusson agreed with Rendall's *transposition of the narration of two stanzas ... and the substitution of milk for wine is essential in the change of setting which the change of language involves. Such liberties are permissible in a "variant" which would not be in what claimed to be a translation.*

Hinmost Days, page 92.
brecks: shallow barren ground   *besooth*: to the south of

Winter Threshing, page 93. December 1947

The Orkney Primula, page 95. 13 January 1947. *The Orkney primula (*Primula Scotica, *but named as a variety* Orcadensis*) is believed by some botanists to have a natural affinity with Scandinavian forms. See note in Spence's* Flora Orcadensis*, pp. 138–9.*

The Kelp-Worker, page 97. 3 January 1947 and 10 August 1947. Rendall described this poem as one of two "near-misses" from *Country Sonnets* (18 August 1947). It was *an attempt to reproduce in verse the kind of thing Millet did in 'The Angelus'; it records, however, an actual experience on the links in Westray that has lived in my mind for years.* The date for this near-miss would be c.1946.

Erling's Rune, page 98. This was inspured by the runic inscriptions inside Maeshowe, the burial chamber. Rendall noted *Ingibjorg the fair widow. Many a woman has bowed her head as she came in here – however an elegant a person she was. ERLINGR,* as being *the actual inscription.*

King Hakon's Dirge, page 99. Early 1948, part of the planned "Sea Symphony". Lament for the King of Norway, whose invading fleet was defeated by the Scots at the Battle of Largs (1263). Making for home, he was ill in Kirkwall for some time, dying there (15 December 1263).

The Moorland Cottage, page 100. The other "near-miss" from *Country Sonnets*, as Rendall wrote on 18 August 1947. The expanded version in the "Newly Collected Poems" section lifts it out of the "slight" category.

The Horse-Mill, page 100. 30 May 1949.

hame: collar

Flight Home, page 102. 2 September 1950. In *Extracts from a Travel Diary 1950*, by Rendall, p23.

Orkney Summer, page 103. 10 June 1947. Following correspondence with James Fergusson, Rendall sent him an "emended' version of the sonnet: *The lone angler together with his pre-Raphelite* [sic] *vocabulary has been decently drowned in the loch and a more realistic if still dreamy and abstract individual substituted!* (18 August 1947).

Lament for the Legends, page 108. While many of the words are not in everyday use, their onomatopoeic quality and the pace of the story make them possible to understand. See also Rendall's note under "Sea Symphony", pages 342–343.

golder: roar
undaemin: extraordinary, huge
sprole: hand-line
treeskie: deceitful, cunning
trow: evil spirit
Tangie: shape-shifting sea-trow
aethic-stane: stone that weights down a net
clett: sea stack

Heather-blether: mythical vanishing island
Vore: Spring
A'm h'ard: I've heard
sweean: burning with pain
tae maet: to feed

SHORE POEMS and other Verse (1957), page 113

To Ernest W. Marwick and other Kirkwall friends with whom I have enjoyed much friendly discussion and criticism.

The original title for this book was *A Season of Calm Weather*, a quotation from Wordsworth, one of Rendall's favourite poets. It was advertised under that title in 1957. In his reply to Tom Scott's letter of 23 January 1965, Rendall suggested: *Although all the poems in it are in English, you might consider that some of them (especially the sonnets) have a Scottish (or should I say an Orcadian?) flavour.*

Lost Self, page 114. 22 May 1954.

Birsay Shore, page 115. 1 August 1952. Original title The Shore. The last stanza of the original was dropped from the book:

> *Against the great sea wall*
> *Which this from that divides*
> *Beat mysterious tides*
> *Deep-ranked along the shore,*
> *Until at last it fall*
> *And Time deceive no more.*

Shore Grave, page 116. 11 February 1953, Birsay.

Morning Wave, page 117. 21 January 1954. Original title Morning wave, Birsay.

Shore Companions, page 119. 1955. Earlier titles were Atlantic Shore and Birds and Beasts.

geo: cleft, sea inlet

In the Ebb, page 120. 1 November 1955. In *The Orkney Herald*, 20 December 1955.

Birsay in Winter, page 121. 10 October and 21 October 1955.

Sea Monsters, page 122. 31 January 1957. Original title, The Strange Land.

The Happy Fisherman, page 123. This was William Harvey, Leabreck, Southside, Birsay.

cuithe: coley   *wand*: rod

Angle of Vision, page 124. 18 October 1956.

Fossils and Fish, page 125. 14 October 1952?

The Stone Wave, page 126. 31 May 1956. Originally
Scupltured in stone, a great Atlantic storm
Holds in this bouldered bay, its wavelike form.

New Cemetery, Birsay, page 126. 24 May 1956. Originally two long lines.

Orkney Historian, page 127. 24 May 1956. That was John Mooney (1862–1950).

A Bygone Kirkwall Gardener, page 127. 24 May 1956. Bob Leitch. Original title Epitaph, etc.

The Miller, page 128. 24 May 1956. Original first two lines; on galleys:
His life was bound by simple wishes
And all his interest bread and fishes.

On Sigurd – WHO GAVE A FIELD AS A GRAVEYARD. page 128. 24 May 1956.

Burgess Ticket, page 129. In *The Orcadian*, 23 December 1954. Hugh Marwick (1881–1965) was being made Freeman of Kirkwall.

Earl Magnus was murdered on Egilsay (1115); his death ended rivalry and civil strife. Earl Rognvald, poet and voyager to the Holy Land, founded St Magnus Cathedral, Kirkwall; died 1158. Sweyn Asleifson was a 12th-century seafarer and warrior.

Jorsalafarers: Jerusalem voyagers, sailing to the Holy Land.

Orkney, page 131. 1955.

Renewal, page 133. 29 December 1953. Apart from George Mackay Brown's essay in *An Orkney Tapestry* (1969), two interesting accounts of this poem's composition are given in letters to Ernest Marwick, from Rendall and Brown.

The Artist, page 134. 14 December 1955.

In Dumfries Museum, page 135. June 1955 and 16 January 1957.

Microcosm of Beauty, page 135. 7 February 1957.

Train Journey, page 136. 23 May 1957; *The Orcadian*, 5 February 1959; in *Extracts from A Travel Diary, 1957–58* (1959).

The Title, page 137. 30 December 1956, 1 a.m.–6 a.m.

Thine Evermore, page 139. c. 30 October 1953. Rendall wrote: *While coming in with the bus last Saturday I wrote (mentally) a few lines that may interest you. Here they are. The first verse seems not too bad.*

His Proper Work, page 141. 27 February 1957.

Without God, page 142. December 1952, *Paterson Church Magazine*.

THE HIDDEN LAND (1966), page 143

In Memory of Edwin

The original title of this book was The Hidden World.

Rendall intended to include the following quotation on the title page:
"... Those shadowy recollections,
Which, be they what they may,
Are yet the fountain-lights of all our days ..."
— Wordsworth

Autumn Sunset, page 144. In *The Glasgow Herald*, 19 October 1963. Harald R. Leslie wrote in *The Orcadian*, 22 February 1979: *At the point of Buckquoy he sat and wrote for me his first draft of a poem "Autumn Sunset in Birsay".*

Marwick Head, page 145. 30 October 1957. The original ending was:
Black reefs of stone or seacliffs ledged and bare
And as I watch your headlands front the flood
Their timeless patience quells my restless blood.

The Encounter, page 146. 22 June and 29 July 1966.

The Sea-Mark, page 147. Part I 4 May 1957; II 20 May 1957. In *The Orcadian*, 5 February 1959 and *Extracts from a Travel Diary, 1957–58* by Rendall (1959); III 14 November 1957.

The Masque, page 149. In *The Glasgow Herald*, 11 June 1959.

The Floss, Westray, page 150. 29 September 1962. In *The Orcadian*, 18 October 1962.

Winter Sadness, page 152. 17 July 1963 and August 1963; printed posthumously in *The Orcadian*, 9 May 1965, in a feature on Rendall.

A Morning at Wasdale, page 153. 1 April 1964.

Bees on Dandelions, page 154. Printed as "The Gleaners" in *The Glasgow Herald*, 27 August 1966.

Evening, page 155. October 1961. In a letter to Hugh Marwick, Rendall described his fascination with haiku, after being given *a small anthology of Japanese in the Haiku tradition … the attempt to use this form in English verse has become with me almost a disease … a grand discipline. Everything must be pictorial, objective, elliptical, express a mood, time and season, have double or even triple images. I send you a few samples.* (8 November 1961.) "Evening" was the first.

Eight O'Clock Bells, page 156. As above.

In Viking Cathedral, page 156. This appeared as "Cathedral Window".

Sunset, Futility, Sea-Fog, Sea Surface, Shipwreck and **Last Obsequies** , *pages 155–156, made up the sequence in* The Hidden Land; although not mentioned in the letter, they are assigned to the early 1960s, given Rendall's absorption with the form.

NEWLY COLLECTED POEMS, page 157

The Sceptic, page 158. 25 October 1947; *The Paterson Church Magazine*, December 1952. Rendall identified it as *Variant on Horace. Ode Bk. I. xxxiv.*

tae vildro: astray

The Morning's Wark, page 159. 27 July 1952. Revised for *The Orcadian*, 13 May 1954. The original version, "Wir Morneen's Wark", had a fourth stanza:
The starfish was a rare een, they tell me,
Nae af'en found,

> *But gied mair pleasure tae Rab*
> *Nor twa pound.*

The Impartial Sun, page 159. 15 April 1967. Rendall wrote: *An epigram in "A Book of Persian Verse" tempted me to write an Orkney variant ... Only – the Persian one had roses and the desert thistle!* Printed in a posthumous feature, *The Orcadian*, 9 May 1968.

The Plastics, page 160. Late 1947? Typed below a typed copy of Douglas Young's "Last Lauch", clearly the model for the spirit and structure of Rendall's poem – one of his unpublished responses to the Synthetic Scots/Lallans/ Plastics debate.

craw nae croose: don't boast

[Fu' o' Bristles], page 160. Another of the same period and, certainly, theme. An important source for the Plastics/ Lallans writers was the famous *Dictionary of the Scottish Language*, by John Jamieson, "abridged by John Johnston, revised edition revised and enlarged by John Longmuir", William P Nimmo, Edinburgh, 1867.

Jeems's Welcome, page 161. The last word, *blide*, can be taken as fond, elliptically expressing affection for the person addressed, *blide [o' you]*, given Rendall's comments on "Doun at the P'lace", page 332.

feenty wird: not a word   *cullya*: gull
cose: swap   *blide*: glad

1920, page 162.
shard: ridge of sand   *heth*: hey

Willie's Boat, page 163. Late June 1966. Rendall's painting, *The Point*, generously lent to us by Mrs Ruth Bain, depicts the boat in the setting described in the poem. Willie/Billy Harvey and his boat appear in other poems by Rendall. The sentiment in this one can be compared with that of "Last Obsequies", on page 156 of this volume.

nile-pin: bilge-plug

Gather Ye Groaties, page 164. Rendall wrote after the poem, *With apologies to Ben*, perhaps substituting Jonson for Herrick, with the latter's *Gather ye Rosebuds* in mind.

breeksed: strained   *coppid*: emptied
gowlan: howling   *cattie buckies*: spiral shellfish

"Mac Pherson o' the Glen", page 165. 1945–46? One of the "Scots' Variations on the Greek Anthology" in fair copy, with a few alterations.

A Bachelor Looks at the Wedding Presents, page 166. 1962. The original fifth stanza was deleted by Rendall:

> *Their home in time will with a cot*
> *Be filled with infant prattle*
> *Then why, O why, has no one thought*
> *To give them both a rattle?*

Showing the "occasional" piece Rendall would produce at social gatherings, anniversaries, weddings, etc. This one was written for his nephew Robert's wedding.

An Orkney Romance, page 168
gluffed: scared   *never leet*: pay no notice

Magnus the Martyr, page 170. Rendall printed this in both the island newspapers: *The Orkney Herald*, 7 April 1926, the present text, and *The Orcadian*, 29 July 1937, the latter with a few slight changes.

On First Seeing 'Linklater and Greig', page 171. 1 January 1947. William Linklater and Robert Greig were famous lifeboatmen and fisherman, who stayed at Yesnaby in huts over the summer. Stanley Cursiter painted them on a rough sea, near the cliffs. The artist was pleased by Rendall's poem, writing on 5 January 1947, *You have caught exactly what I had in mind when the picture was painted.* Cursiter was lavish in his praise of Rendall, employing similar imagery elsewhere: *You catch the essence of Orkney* (3 December 1946); *You have caught* (as above) and *You have captured the very essence of the Orkney scene* (27 September 1947).

Motor Run to Birsay October 1949, page 172. October 1949? and 1 March 1951.

Birsay in Winter, page 173. 1955.

Tradition, page 173. 24 May 1956.

Plane Crash in Hoy, page 174. 1 April 1954. Revised 15 February 1957.

In Birsay, page 175. 9 January 1959. William Soutar and Edwin Muir were the poets mentioned. Printed in *The Orkney Herald*, 13 January 1959.

A Day in Kirkwall, 1759, page 176. 27 October 1959.

Birsay Sunset, page 176. Among the "samples" of Rendall's experiments with the haiku form on 8 November 1961, sent to his friend Stanley Cursiter, this poem is dated a short time before that.

Orkney Sunset, page 177. 2 October 1963; revised 25 October 1963.

The View, page 177. 18 November 1964.

Prehistoric Monster, page 178. On 7 November 1966, Rendall sent Ernest Marwick *4 new haiki (must we invent a plural!)*, this poem and "Derelict Cottage", "Portrait" and "Stromness". In a later version he renamed the second poem "Derelict Cottage, Pierowall".

Sunset [2], page 179. 1966–67. Very interested in haiku, Rendall had many attempts at economy and precision within the form. Compare this poem with the variant on page 321.

The Wreck, page 179. On 15 January 1967, Rendall wrote of *... the wreck on the Kirk Skerries ... an impulse to do a poem on the same theme* [as Ian MacInnes's painting, which Rendall admired]. *I have attempted it in the classical Sapphic metre – rhymeless but with due care of "quantity" in the syllabic pattern ... Today I have posted the poem on "The Wreck" to the Editor of the Scots Magazine for possible acceptance by that periodical.* It had been after some trouble that he did so: *I've wrestled with my new poem and have more or less finished (for the meantime) its final form. The intractable first line of the third stanza now runs*
  Soon, come storm or calm, will the dauntless vessel ...
(11 January 1967, 2 a.m. – to Ernest Marwick). His first draft was dated 6 January 1967.

Stromness [2], page 180. In *The Orcadian*, 16 February 1967.

The Bay, Birsay, page 180. 31 January 1957.

Orkney Sunset [2], page 182. 2 October 1963.

Orkney's Beauty, page 182. In *The Kirkwallian*, No. 14, New Series, July 1932.

Evening Watch, Scapa Flow, page 183. 1917–18, on HMS *Imperieuse*, the ship on which Rendall served, as a steward in the officers' mess.

Orkney After the War, page 183. 26 December 1946. See note on p350, "Ebb Tide".

On Air, page 184. 1917, HMS *Imperieuse. Influence. Returning towards Kirkwall on Ayre Road on fine summer day.* (Note by Rendall.)

Evening's Casement, page 184. 1918, HMS *Imperieuse. Influence. Memory of fine sunset over Kirkwall Bay.* (Note by Rendall.)

Costa Head, page 185. *The Orkney Herald*, 21 April 1926.

Early Snow, page 185. The best of three manuscript efforts.

The Shepherd, page 187. 28 November 1958.

Abbey Craigs, page 187. 28 March 1926. In *The Kirkwallian*, No. 8, New Series, January 1927.

Written after Reading Matthew Arnold's Poems, page 188. 14 and 24 December 1926.

To the Nightingale, page 189. 14 January 1927.

The Barefoot Maiden, page 189. 25 January 1927.

Sea Anemone, page 192. 1916–17, *There is a beauty, a Dahlia. I address it thus.* Rendall in work for English Composition / Evening Continuation Class, Kirkwall Burgh School, Session 1916–1917. In "Island Marine Jungle", *The Glasgow Herald*, 9 February 1952, Rendall described how *Sea-anemones, deceptive tropical flowers whose beauty lures but to sting and devour, wave their tentacles.*

Rosa Excelsa, page 192. 1917, HMS *Imperieuse. Influence. Consideration of natural and mental possessions.* (Note by Rendall.)

To a Sea-Gull, page 193. July 1925. *The Kirkwallian*, New Series, July 1925.

To a Speedwell, page 196. 1918, HMS *Imperieuse*. Rendall was pleased by the comments and advice he received about three poems he had sent to *Great Thoughts*, a prestigious literary periodical. The poems were "To a Speedwell", "Faith, Hope and Charity" and "On the Prospect of Distant Hills". The response to his submission was first in the Replies section, 16 February 1918.

Evening, page 197. Summer, 1926.

Cerithium, page 197. 15 February 1948.

Distance, page 198. 7 February 1957.

Bird's-eye View, page 198. 15 and 19 December 1959.

Spring Equinox, page 199. 4 February 1955.

Address to a Sea Anemone, page 199. 21 December 1959.

The Palmist, page 200. 22 October 1953, London. Rendall wrote: *...some wonderful sights over the Alps and looking right down into great basins between the mountains scored with glaciers, ringed with snow peaks.*

[The Skyline of Eternity], page 201. 5 November 1923.

Daily Edition, page 203. *The Orcadian*, 10 November 1954.

[Not by Bread Alone], page 204. 17 May 1949.

To Myself I Say, page 205. 1916–17, in evening class work, an essay, "Soliloquy on an Orkney Shore".

The Purpose, page 205. 1917?, HMS *Imperieuse. Influence. The appeal of Hay Hills from Brims.* (Note by Rendall.)

The Soul's Reply, page 207. 1917, HMS *Imperieuse*. Revised 20 February 1918. *Influence. Thoughts on the characteristics of Heaven.* (Note by Rendall.)

Out of the Depths, page 208. 20 February 1920.

The Response, page 210. 10 November 1920. (Reply to the previous poem.)

[Lengthen not the Inward Strife], page 212. 21 October 1920.

On Giving, page 213. 1918, HMS *Imperieuse. Influence. Reading a sermon on Christian giving.* (Note by Rendall.)

Faith, page 214. 1917, HMS *Imperieuse*.

Paul's Preaching, page 214. Christmas 1974.

Paul in Prison, page 215. January 1924.

To an Engraving of Bishop Reynolds, page 216. 4 March 1925.

Christ Risen, page 217. January 1924; *The Orkney Herald*, 30 September 1925.

The Soul's Deliverance, page 218. 6 June 1926; *The Orkney Herald*, 9 June 1926.

The Miracle, page 219. 25 February 1927; *The Orkney Herald*, 4 May 1927.

[Leaving Northbank], page 220. 28 February 1953. Compare the image in the last few lines of "Winter Mood", *Country Sonnets*, page 49.

A Christian's Couplets in Time of War, page 221. July 1940.

Princely Offerings, page 222. March 1952.

Between the Tidemarks, page 223. 14 and 17 October 1952.

The Floods Came, page 224. 5 February 1953, in *The Orcadian*.

The Ordeal, page 224. 18 October 1954.

The Chief Butler, page 225. 14 November 1954.

The Riddle, page 226. 31 January 1959. Two stanzas of a version dated 16 January were deleted from the later one:

> *Quite bemused, I turn until*
> *I light on Wyre's simple isle,*
> *Lest aught be there discovered still*
> *Where Edwin sat upon the hill*
> *"Not yet," she whispers with a smile.*
>
> *North Ronaldsay – she seems to stand*
> *Aloof in private reverie,*
> *As if she held within her hand*
> *Treasured gold as contraband.*
> *She answers, "It is not in me."*

The Beautiful Feet, page 227. 7, 8 and 10 June 1963. *Begun in Piazza Maggiore, Bologna, on 7th June, finished on Cross Channel steamer and revised at Berkhamsted.* (Note by Rendall.)

On the Cross, page 228. 19 June 1966, Aberdeen Assembly Hall. Rendall wrote from Mitchell Ward, Royal Cornhill Hospital, Aberdeen, on 4 July 1966: *I've had a poem accepted by "The Witness"! Here is the poem based on a verse in Ps 118, 'They compassed me about like bees'*; *The Witness*, 97/11 (November 1966).

Gifts and Glory, page 229. 9 December 1966. Written, by request, for the Adventurers, a Stromness Youth Group.

One Flock, page 230. 1954? (Same typeface and paper as 'The Ordeal' (18 October 1954).

Rackwick, Hoy, page 233. 7 January 1947.

A Disciple Speaks, page 234. 18 September to 9 October 1960.

The Imperishable Thing, page 235. Stanza 1 was the first in "The Praise of Beauty", in *Country Sonnets*, page 60.

Lord and Christ, page 236. 23 October 1953.

Home Thoughts, page 237. 1917, HMS *Imperieuse. Influence. Separation of family on Xmas-day.* (Note by Rendall.)

The Pirate's Grave, page 237. 2 July 1927.

The Yacht Sings, page 238. c.13 September 1957.

The Boy and the Daisy, page 238. 12 August 1957, Westray. Compare 'As a Boy in a Field', page 241.

[Apocalypse], page 239. 30 October 1957.

Dream Procession, page 239. 7 August 1965, Balfour Hospital, Kirkwall.

Convalescence, page 240. 22 June 1960, Royal Cornhill Hospital, Aberdeen.

As a Boy in a Field, page 241. 6 January 1967. Compare 'The Boy and the Daisy', page 238.

On a London Street, page 241. May 1967. In *The Orcadian*, 15 June 1967: *Just a fortnight before he died, when already very ill,*

Robert Rendall wrote the following poem, inspired by a memory of seeing on a London street many years ago slum children returning from the country with hands filled with wild flowers.

The Peat Worker, page 242. 4 February 1943, on the back of "The Shepherds", in *Country Sonnets*, of that date.

tusker: peat spade

The Poet, page 242. Self-portrait.

The Sea-Wall, page 243. Rendall spent much time on different starts, changes ... without dating them. "The old sea-wall" is a recurrent reference in his work.

Four Bells, page 247. 1917? Fair copy, in writing the same as the HMS *Imperieuse* poems.

'rattle': 'on report'

The Return from Innisfree, page 248. 28 February 1910. Rendall later revised this parody of W. B. Yeats's much parodied poem

The Tragedy, page 249. 21–28 May 1927; in *The Kirkwallian*, No. 9, New Series, December 1927.

The Reef, page 252. Late 1966?

Life, page 253. 1926–27.

Frolic in the Stratosphere, page 254. 16 June 1928. Original title Sol the Sailorman.

The Devil's Thimble, page 256. 5 November 1927.

Winter, page 258. 1918–26. These last four stanzas were dropped from the original version, not appearing in *Country Sonnets*.

Midsummer Night, page 261. 22–28 November 1959

A Little Hillside Lane, page 262. 20 June 1927.

The Brocken, page 263. 5 November 1927.

A Cliff Conversation, page 265. First stanza, early 1964. A second stanza completed the poem on 9 November 1964.

Tammy-norries: puffins   *scarfie*: cormorant
scorries: young gulls

On Boardhouse Loch, page 266. One of Rendall's most extensively worked and corrected poems. Some versions have, for lines 4–6 of stanza 2:

Showed such diversity and grace.
I stood entranced
Then with hushed breath…

Imitations, page 267. 7 November 1966. Subtitled *(for an artist's daughter)*, when his portrait was being painted.

The Flood-Tide, page 268. 24 December 1924.

Sea Symphony, page 269. Rendall had been working on what he called *this theme-poem*, in the late 1940s, but was discouraged by James Fergusson's blunt assertion that Rendall was a *lyric* poet. Rendall did not abandon the project, but did little to it in the way of promoting interest or filling out the outline he sketched after completing a substantial part of his plan to present the sweep of Orkney's history, narrative punctuated by lyrics – some fine passages make it worth printing, we feel. In a "scenario" for the poem – which included some lyrics in print, Rendall asserted: *Everything is within our radius – sky, land and ocean (This is our land of heritage) and we its tenantry.*

The mythical creatures are identified in Rendall's note:

Nuckelavee is an authentic local water-horse, and the description quite accurate, as verified by those who have seen him!

The Mester (or Muckle) Stoor-Worm is our brand of sea-serpent, and old tales are preserved of how he was slain by Assipattle who valiantly sailed down his throat in a small boat, and set fire to his liver, thereby causing its death. In its convulsions it bit out its forked tongue which is still seen as the Baltic Sea, and several of its teeth, as witness the existence of the Orkneys and the Shetlands, and the last plunge of the monster into the ocean was somewhere up about Iceland, where the proof of the whole story is still valid – the smoke and flames still come up!

The Mester ship is an old legend, and there are lots of far-fetched stories recorded about it, too long to detail here. It once left two sailors up aloft in the moon after the accident referred to.

The Sea-mither gives birth to the swarming life of the seas and reigns throughout the summer, following the Vore-tullye or Spring equinox, when Terran, the giant, is overcome, and consigned to the floor of the ocean, where, however, he still struggles, as witness the storms even in summer! But he breaks loose in the Gore-tullye, and has a time of it all winter, forcing the Sea-mither to fly for her life.

Italian Funeral, page 278. 6–7 February 1957. Rendall wrote a vivid description of the event which inspired the poem, in *Extracts from A Travel Diary 1957–58* (1959).

Italian Funeral [2], page 280. This shorter treatment is of the same theme and date.

rimpled: wrinkled

[Blind when a Boy], page 281.
ware: kind of seaweed

Spring 1947, page 282. Spring, 1947.

Departure, page 283. 12 September–1 October 1947.

In Memory of Sir William Wallace, page 285. Summer, 1926.

Ode of Welcome to Her Majesty Queen Elizabeth, page 286. Original version 20 February 1959. Prepared on card with a few slight changes, nearer the time of the Queen's projected visit to Orkney. That official visit inspired Rendall to an "official" poem in laureate mode – like "Sea Symphony" – but in the event it was not delivered publicly because Her Majesty's confinement entailed cancellation of engagements.

Born 1854 [extract], page 288. 1954. Extract from a long poem in celebration of *The Orcadian* newspaper's centenary.

spoots: razor-shells

The Farmer, page 289. 22 January 1930.

The Farewell Sting, page 291. 15 October 1957. *I got badly stung by a wasp. My wrist still 'swees' from that ... to pass the time I write some nonsense verses and entitle them: THE FAREWELL STING!* (Rendall's *Extracts from A Travel Diary 1957–58*.)

swees: smarts

Hogmanay 1928, page 292. 31 December 1928.

Poet Myopicus, page 293.

   scorrie: young gull   *Tammy-norrie*: puffin

[Curly Kail], page 294. 1947–48? Rendall used Wordsworth's "Scorn not the Sonnet" (1827) as the model for this attack on the "Plastics".

Limericks, page 294. The Italian for "wedding" is *sposalizio*. *dundies*: coley   *partan*: crab

Hogmanay, page 296. One of Rendall's verse-advertisements for the drapery firm.

Coupon-Free, page 297. Another verse-advertisement.

Yule-tide at the Bridge, page 298. *The Orkney Herald*, 8 December 1926.

The Armada of 1588, page 302. 1915. Verse-advertisement for "The Armada 1588 and Xmas 1915 Exhibition". Rendall did many of them, imitating the styles of poets, established classics and talents of his own lifetime. Frequently very long, they would take up considerable space on page 1 of a newspaper, catching the eye and, by their pastiches of Longfellow, Brooke, Stevenson, the Ballads and many others, providing entertainment while the "message" was communicated. One of the earliest of Rendall's compositions in this mode.

The Battle of Kirkwall Bridge, page 303. Spring, 1915. Written in a boyish hand, this seems likely to be earlier than the poem just noted. Since Rendall had drawn up plans for displaying goods in appropriate units, with illustrations, it is likely that he would approach a verse-project with confidence.

Rendall's Bazaar, page 304. We think this is the best of his verse-advertisements, amusing, metrically accomplished, placing the goods and prospective customers' attitudes in a contemporary context, while the echoes of Antony's words and tactics are adroitly successful.

Brig News, page 308.
feelie dyke: turf wall   *rugsing*: tugging

Art and Appetite, page 310. 16 April 1948. *The Glasgow Herald*. Not signed, but kept among his papers. Given his friendship with Stanley Cursiter and correspondence with James Fergusson, it seems to us that the "skit" could hardly be by anyone else.

Si Deus Nobiscum, page 311. c.1911? In a young hand, this piece dwells upon the Kirkwall Burgh School's motto. That he kept it for so many years testifies to Rendall's authorship. It is thought that this must be his earliest poem. Some lines are illegible because the original manuscript is very badly creased.

[Life's Supremest Good is Won], page 313. We date this, 17 May 1949, comparing the four lines to the conclusion of the sonnet, "[Not by Bread Alone]", page 204. Both passages have a sententiously kindly and practical ring. It may be that "[Life's Supremest Good is Won]" was an attempt at a conclusion to the sonnet. (There are many examples of apparently free-standing verse in Rendall's papers that turn out to have been efforts at texts before and after he had dated and signed them off.)

[The Islands], page 313. A working typescript. These lines seem to be all that is "finished" and coherent.

Epithalamium [extract], page 314. Part of an amusing "occasional" piece, long and well-sustained. Rendall noted that an epithalamium was *A song or poem celebrating a marriage.*

A Farewell Address [extract], page 315. Printed, as it suggests something of the society Rendall enjoyed in Kirkwall – friends, conversation, various creative and domestic activities in which several gifted people engaged. The occasion was Ernest Marwick and his wife Janette's leaving for Newbattle, where Ernest was to study in the wake of George Mackay Brown.

An Old English Manor, page 315. Another look at "Scottish or English" writing and the associated "camps".

Auld Reekie: Edinburgh

Sent, page 316. Two words cannot be deciphered from this manuscript, folded and left for so long that it is very heavily creased. The title was within inverted commas.

[Through Thicket, Bracken and Thorn], page 317. Another passage worth preserving, with regret that it seems to have been scribbled down while Rendall was working at another text.

A Country Burial [extra], page 318. 11 February 1929. This concluding section was omitted from the version in *Country Sonnets*.

The Night Wind, page 319. 1918–26. These are the last four stanzas of the poem, omitted from the *Country Sonnets* version.

Departure [fourth stanza], page 319. 1 October 1947. A new opening stanza was provided, making the original one stanza 2:

> *My friend! – ah, thou art gone!*
> > *No more for thee*
> > *Morning's delight may be;*
> *The silver-mantled dawn*
> > *Is not for thee.*

The original stanza 4 was deleted:

> > *No, not for thee*
> *Night's treasures are displayed,*
> > *Not now for thee*
> > *Sparkles her jewelry,*
> *Like gems on violet laid.*

Death, page 320. A "restoration". First version of "The Moorland Cottage", published in *Orkney Variants*. It followed "Life" in a book of fair copies. Although *a near-miss* for *Country Sonnets*, as Rendall described it, the shorter text is inferior to the original.

Stromness [2] [first and fourth stanzas], page 321. 1966–67. Giving examples of how Rendall worked on his poems, these are variations of stanzas of the poem on page 180. An alternative for 'uprear' in the third of these examples was 'uprose'. Alternatives for 'And on' in the fourth example were 'Upon' and 'Over'. He also rewrote the material in haiku form; see page 178.

Sunset [3], page 321. 1966–67. Compare with the poem on page 179.

Ebb Tide, page 322. 26 December 1946. This seems to us to be the better of two versions of this date. While there are obvious correspondences between this poem's theme and treatment and those aspects of "Orkney After the War", page 183 above, we print both texts. Several changes illustrate Rendall's habit of seeking to improve work that many readers would have regarded as successful.

buckies: spiral shellfish

A Cliff Conversation, page 322. A second section, dated 9 November 1964, completes the poem.

scarfies: cormorants

Rule Thou in Majesty Divine, page 323. Original title Hymn (Wisdom, strength and praise unending...). Given the present title on 4 June 1936.

On an Engraving [second stanza], page 324. This is an alternative second stanza of "To an Engraving of Bishop Reynolds", of the same date, 4 March 1925.